Think Before You Write

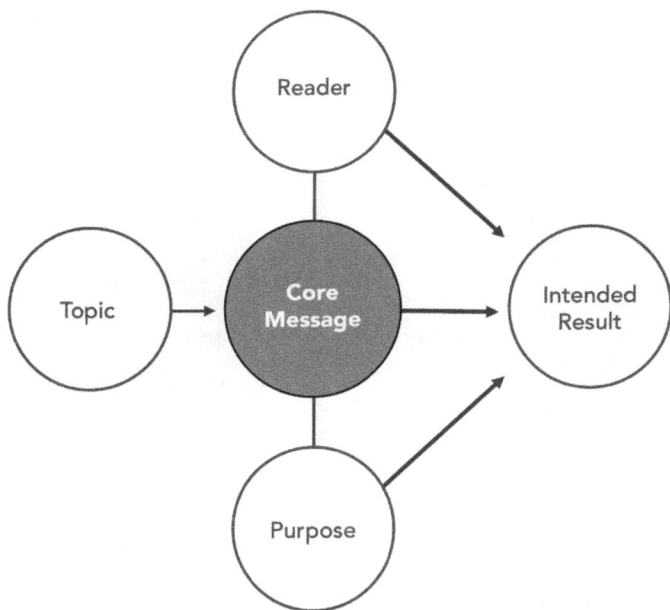

Reader

Topic → Core Message → Intended Result

Purpose

**plan, organize, and build
professional documents
with precision**

PETER INGLE

Library of Congress Cataloging-in-Publication Data

Ingle, Peter M.
Think Before You Write

ISBN 978-0-9746349-0-6

Produced in the United States

REVISED

✪

Plans are worthless,
but planning is everything.

Dwight D. Eisenhower

Think Before You Write

Foreword

When I started as a business writer, I searched for books about what to do and how to do it. I found scant information beyond the well-worn formula of:

(1) outline

(2) write

(3) edit

Meanwhile, the business world was exploding with new concepts of total quality management and agile software development, both of which stress continuous improvement.

I started incorporating those and other ideas in a new method of building documents *in stages* with a strong emphasis on thorough planning before ever writing a single sentence. I called this method 'strategic content development' and I started giving workshops about it.

Those workshops became the basis for this book.

Think Before You Write

CONTENTS

Be a Strategic Writer

Put things in order before they exist.
Lao Tzu

Plan with Purpose

Most people cannot explain their writing process because they don't have one. They simply throw together a loose outline and start writing. They don't take time to design an underlying structure that supports and reflects their strategy. As a result, they fail to build a foundation on which they could easily assemble content. Their writing ends up lacking the integrity of architecture, the surety of engineering, and the clarity of a core message—and readers are affected by the lack of all three.

Don't let this happen to you. Instead, take time to align your creativity and planning with a clear strategy *before* you write so that you can execute with confidence, direction, and precision as you write.

Ideally, nothing should be left out during initial planning. You want to be certain about every ingredient in your message, why you are including it, where it best fits in your message, and what effect you want to have on the reader at each step. It used to be said that you need a strong beginning and a strong ending, and even better is when you also have a strong middle. But the truth is that you want your document to be strong at *every* paragraph and *every* sentence. But it cannot happen by itself. You have to be ready to put in the effort to make it work.

Build a Strong Core

The main thing to pin down before you assemble your written ingredients is the core message that will tie them together and unify them for the reader. Surprisingly, the core message of many documents is either missing or hard to find. Why? Because the writer's planning was inadequate. Too much energy was spent on a general concept of what *they felt they wanted to say.* Not enough time was devoted to being specific about the core message that *needed to be delivered* and the best way to deliver it to the reader.

You cannot underestimate the importance of knowing your core message. Pinning it down so that you really know it and understand it will also confirm why you are delivering and what effect you want it to have. When you can do state your core message in one sentence (the briefer the better), and if you can build around this core as you write, your message will be well on its way to clarity, impact, and success.

Pinpointing your core message sounds easy, but it is rarely easy because it requires the dedicated work of pondering, conceiving, pruning, distilling, sharpening, and polishing *exactly* what you want to convey *before* you start writing. Can your message find clarity as you write? Yes, because new things are always discovered and revealed as you write. However, your message can find come to even better clarity if it starts out already clear.

✪ Strategic writing involves (1) building your message around a central core and (2) organizing all your content for impact for the purpose of (3) delivering your message to achieve a specific, predetermined result.

Define Each Element of Your Topic

To communicate your message well, you have to have a firm grasp of all the elements related to your topic. Here are some definitive questions to ask as the first stage of planning:

- What is my main topic?

- Who is the specific, ideal reader?

- What is the purpose behind writing this document?

- What specific result(s) do I want to achieve?

- What is the central, core message I want to send?

If you want your message to be successful, you cannot have a vague idea about any of these points. You need to scrutinize each of them and nail down exactly why and how each of them is important. You cannot afford for any of them to be vague. You cannot leave any of them to guesswork or hope.

The more command you have of these elements, the more confidence and control you will have before you start writing. When all of them are clear in your mind, you will feel sure that you can impact the reader the way you intend, according to your purpose. You will also have a clear, reliable blueprint to keep aligning with as you write. This does not mean that you have set a rigid course that will stifle your creativity, spontaneity, and insight. On the contrary, it means you will have a well conceived backdrop against which all three of these can play themselves out freely and safely without undermining or misdirecting your original intent.

✪ It takes practice to dissect and think through a topic each time you write. Be definite. Write down your response to each of the bullets above. Take time to mull them over. Keep clarifying them and sharpening them and simplifying them as much as possible before you jump into writing.

✪ In the planning stages, think of yourself as an artist doing several preliminary sketches before committing to the canvas, or as an architect letting your insights find their way into informal pencil drawings before they become part of a final blueprint.

Analyze Each Element

Elements of a topic

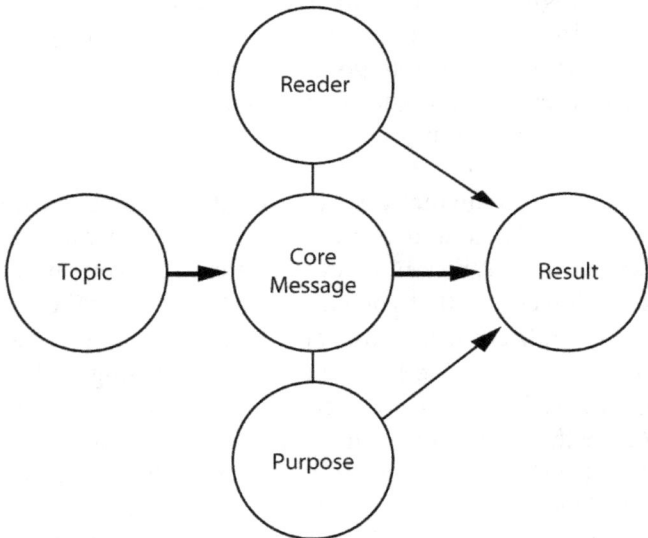

Reader

Topic → Core Message → Result

Purpose

This simple tool can be extremely helpful as you plan and as you write. It is your big-picture strategy of what you want to deliver, why, to whom, how, and why. It is also easy to sketch on a simple piece of paper as a predecessor to your more formal mind map.

Below are some guidelines to help you get specific about the five key elements that should be a part of your planning for any type and size of document.

What is the main topic?

What exactly are you writing about or trying to say? What is the context, the background? Don't think about your title. Think about the substance and meaning of your topic. For example, the title might be 'Lexus' whereas the topic is really 'the world's most luxurious automobile'. Look beneath the label (which is what a topic is) and try to articulate what it is that you want your message to represent. What is the essence of your message? And remember that your message is not necessarily something concrete you have to tell the reader. It is what you want your message to convey. It is what you want to feel certain about as the strategic foundation underlying your message. Roses and pearls and diamonds often con-vey a stronger message with more lasting impact than the words, 'I love you'.

Who is the ideal reader?

Effective speakers speak to individuals, not to groups. In their mind's eye, they talk to the one ideal person they want to reach. They are not trying to appeal to or satisfy everyone's expectations. Rather, they are intending that each person sitting in the audience is their one ideal 'customer'. This is what you want to do when you write.

When you write to the ideal reader of your message, your message gets delivered with greater purpose and impact.

What is the purpose behind writing this document?

Why are you writing? Do you want to inform, in-struct, entertain, inspire, persuade? Being absolutely certain about your purpose helps establish the strate-gy, the direction, and the tone of every sentence and paragraph you write. Readers don't just appreciate this; they want a message that follows a consistent direction and clear goal.

What result(s) do I want to achieve??

What do you want the reader to do? Learn some-thing, feel something, do something, buy something? The more definitive you are about what you want the reader to achieve, the more successfully you will evoke that result in the reader. And even though the reader is your initial target, it is this final intended result that you are really after.

✪ Your audience is the reader/customer, but your true target is the intended result. You are trying to strategical-ly strike the former to achieve the latter.

✪ Many writers get caught up in what they are saying, or distracted by who they are saying it to, and lose sight of the result they want their message to achieve.

What is the central, core message?

Most importantly, what are you delivering? What critical thing do you want to convey? What main thing do you want the reader to know? What idea or theme is at the heart of your topic and common to your entire message or document? What is the unify-ing element that ties everything else together in a clear way? Once the reader steps away, what is the lasting impression or response that you want implanted in his or her mind?

✪ Writers—particularly in the ad industry—may be tempted to be clever with their message and how they deliver it, and as a result can end up standing in the way of their intended result. One example of this is the now fashionable technique of making a strong selling point and then following it with a clever or humorous twist that 'tickles' the reader's response. What happens all too often, however, is that the tickle turns readers' minds and emotions in a differ-ent direction; so much so that the selling point (and even the product name) gets erased from their mind.

✪ Making a message clever rather than clear can cause it to collapse, disappear, and be forgotten.

The Importance of Your Core Message

Your core message is like the core of an apple or the hub of a wheel. Everything else is tied to it and depends on it. It should link all the elements of your communication and roll them out smoothly to the reader while keeping the focus on the core.

For any communication to come alive, it needs to be converted into a clear message. To achieve this, it needs to be infused with your central idea, your purpose for delivering it, and your intended result on the reader. What (topic) are you saying, why (purpose) are you say-ing it, and how (result) do you want it to specifically impact the reader? If you can incorporate all of these elements into your core message, it will strike the target every time.

It sounds simple, and it is, but it is not easy to find the core of your message. You have to turn your topic inside-out, distill your thinking, and hone your intention until you can state the core message in one sentence—all of which takes time and concentration. The reward, however, is that the more clearly and concisely you pin down the core before you write, the sharper your writing will be and the more exacting your target will be.

If you have trouble pinpointing your core message, try to define the problem your document will solve, then enunciate the solution. Here is one example:

Problem
Most forms of written communication fail because they lack a clear message, a clear strategy for delivering it, and a solid foundation for executing it.

Solution
Plan and organize your message around a clear core, then build all other content in strategic stages around the core.

Core Message
Think Before You Write.

✪ Distilling your core message is not as easy as this example may make it seem. Each kind and size of project is different, and it may take hours or days or longer to brainstorm, experiment, and fine-tune your bow-and-arrow tool. Remember, however, that if you are struggling with your core message, you will struggle when writing—because you will still be searching for the core.

✪ If you gloss over this stage or move through it too quickly, you will be starting on a vague foundation that will render your writing weak and ineffective no matter how glorious your sentences may be. Behind them something critical will be missing, and your readers will feel it.

Filling Out the Bow-and-Arrow Diagram

You have a message you want to deliver and a target you want to hit. To strike the bull's eye (to achieve your intended result), you need to concentrate on the pivot point (your central message) and sharpen your aim by balancing the two ends of your bow (your reader and your purpose). The more all these elements synchronize and align, the better your shot will be. And you will feel it: the certainty will bolster your sense of confidence and direction.

✪ Think of the bow-and-arrow process as pre-writing. It is still writing—you are writing down ideas and moving them around—but you are using a unique mindset that is big-picture focused and distinct from the kind of expressive, explanatory writing you will use later when crafting the content.

Having an Image of the Whole

An often overlooked value of the bow-and-arrow tool is that it helps you establish a single view of the larger whole. Being able to keep this picture in your mind while writing can be an invaluable aid and compass. Most writers know how easy it is to run off course or get caught up in a sudden, tangential idea. The bow-and-arrow tool helps you stay on target and aligned.

Bow and arrow tool

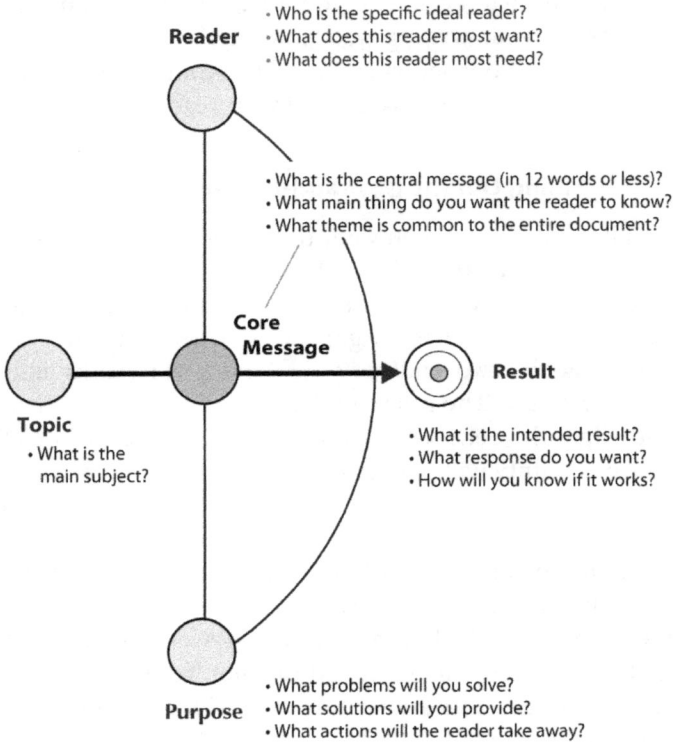

Reader
- Who is the specific ideal reader?
- What does this reader most want?
- What does this reader most need?

- What is the central message (in 12 words or less)?
- What main thing do you want the reader to know?
- What theme is common to the entire document?

Core Message

Result

Topic
- What is the main subject?

- What is the intended result?
- What response do you want?
- How will you know if it works?

Purpose
- What problems will you solve?
- What solutions will you provide?
- What actions will the reader take away?

Plan Backwards?

When it comes to planning, does the order of your five key elements matter? It may, but you can also play with it. For instance, instead of thinking in the sequence of topic, reader, purpose, core, and result, you can start with your intended result and pin *that* down, then establish the core message, and from there break down your purpose, who the ideal reader is, and what the general topic should be. This can keep your thinking dynamic.

Pitfalls to Watch For

As you plan and prepare to write, keep in mind the following temptations that lie in wait ready to derail every writer:

- **Don't rush planning**. It is easy to skip or rush planning and jump into writing. But without careful planning, your writing will lack clarity, purpose, and strength. Everyone wants to start writing right away, and often their clients and bosses also want them to start writing, but it is a mistake that is rife with other mistakes which are sure to follow.

  ✪ One of the best things you can do is get consensus from *all* team members that planning deserves time, that diving into writing is not a legitimate sign of progress, and that careful planning is going to enhance the writing and produce a better result.

- **Don't write for a broad audience**. A large audience isolates you as the writer. It also dilutes your message and weakens its delivery. Explaining your message to one ideal reader forces you to know *what* the message really is. Envisioning just one reader incites you to understand *why* you want to achieve a certain result, and forces you to be definitive about *how* your solution will work.

  ✪ It may seem silly at first, but your document will gain a lot of strength if you pretend you are writing it for and to one person. You can even give this imagined ideal reader a name and profile of someone with specific needs.

- **Minimize rewriting**. Extensive rewriting is a symptom of poor planning. Something has to make up for poor planning and rewriting is usually the unwelcome victim. Extensive rewriting also leads to extensive editing (the next victim).

✪ Rewriting and editing can *never* replace planning. Superior writing derives from superior planning.

- **Don't worry about style.** Focusing too much on how you sound (style) prevents you from delivering what you want to say (a clear message). Keep in mind that the reader is far more interested in the message than in you and your style. The truth is that readers—in the business world especially—don't want to wade through and fight with a lot of text to get what they need. They want you to deliver the message as clearly and quickly as possible.

Standards to Aim For

The remedy to the pitfalls described above is to adopt and encourage the following standards as part of your team-writing strategy and methodology:

- **Organize your structure before you start writing.** Resist the urge to start writing. Step back. Focus your thinking lens. Knead the dough of your message before putting it in the oven. The more you clarify your message, purpose, and result, the more control you will have when you write. Remember, too, that good planning benefits you *and* the reader.

✪ Don't limit 'sketching' to just the bow-and-arrow planning phase. You can also sketch sections and even paragraphs before you flesh them out with full writing. Doing so is a way to be sure you capture key points before getting lost in explaining them.

- **Write for a specific reader.** Speak to the one reader you feel most wants and needs your message. This will sharpen your focus, clarify your message, and give your writing a firm tone. You can also ask yourself: Is this a document that would serve my needs? Would *I* want to read it? How would I feel after reading it? What effect or call-to-action would it prompt in me?

  ✪ Ask someone not associated with the project to read your first draft and tell you what they understand from it; then match their feedback with your bow-and-arrow and ask yourself, did the plan work? How might it be improved? Made more clear? Made more simple and direct?

- **Separate writing and editing.** Writing is the development of ideas. Editing is realignment and polish. When these are not preceded by good planning, however, they become simply band aids for poor organization, and they end up interfering with each other. Many writers don't even realize, while editing, that they are struggling with their own lack of planning and organization.

  ✪ Thorough planning leads to integrous organization, which guides clear writing, which leads to simple editing.

- **Focus on the core message.** *The task of writing is to deliver a razor-sharp message to the reader.* When you are absolutely certain about your message, a tone of certainty will ring clear and give natural shape to your writing. Always hold firm to your core message.

Cautions About Poor Planning

Remember that poor planning makes the entire writing process harder. When you hurry planning and jump into writing, your document becomes a jungle of words in which writer, reader, and message all get lost.

Planning is often rushed or skipped because it is hard work. It seems much easier to just start writing—to get words on paper—because that creates the *impression* that you are getting something done. It is a classic mistake.

Unfortunately, most of us were never shown how to plan before writing. We were not taught the necessity of a core message, how to establish a direction for our communication, or how to organize our message for the reader's benefit. Instead we learned—and have come to take for granted—the oversimplified approach of: (1) make a quick outline, (2) write a rough draft, (3) revise and edit.

This 3-step approach is like trying to build a pyramid upside-down. It creates a top-heavy load that makes your document unstable. It also makes each stage of writing more time consuming than the previous one because words accumulate with no foundation, no structure, no direction, and no core.

A lack of solid construction also leads to extensive rewriting and editing in an attempt to fix an unclear or fragmented message. But rewriting and editing *can never repair an unstable foundation.* The only way is to go back and build a proper foundation, if you know how.

Avoid an Unstable Foundation

A lack of planning guarantees that you will struggle to gain control of your document as you write. If you build on an unstable foundation—illustrated below—the process of writing is going to become an unwieldy cycle of repetitive rewriting, reorganizing, and editing. It can also cause your document to collapse or implode.

Unstable process

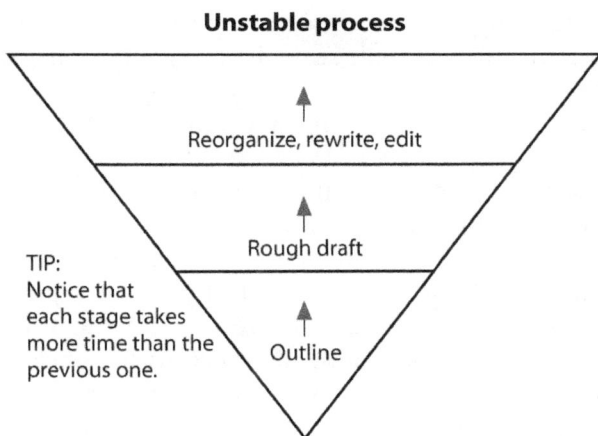

Reorganize, rewrite, edit

Rough draft

TIP:
Notice that
each stage takes
more time than the
previous one.

Outline

Without strategic planning, your writing process is doomed to unfold in the following way: as you write, the lack of a clear message will force you into rewriting; rewriting will reveal that the document's structure is unstable; and you will be forced to backtrack to reorganizing—which you will have to do with more rewriting. Each stage, instead of building toward the next, will become a struggle to clean up the previous stage. But it never really works, which is why written communication so often fails to accomplish its task of delivering a succinct message to the reader according to a strategy for impacting the reader.

Tips For Good Planning

Your goal is to stay focused on the core message as you write. You want to engineer and build progressive stages of a concept, a foundation, a structure, and a body that all echo and reinforce your core message.

Anyone who has watched a high-rise being built knows that a lot of time passes before the building is visible. Months go by before the structure springs into existence. And after it does, people see only the exterior. They forget about the foundation and they are oblivious to how the structure was put together and why it matters.

The same is true of a written document that has been planned and built strategically. All your efforts of thinking, sketching, and outlining may not produce complete sentences and paragraphs until halfway into a project, and the reader will eventually see only your message— not its blueprint, foundation, or structure. But once your foundation and structure are established, each stage of construction will reinforce the next, and all you will have to do is concentrate on delivering a clear message.

✪ The key is to remember that until you establish (1) your purpose for writing, (2) the result you intend to achieve, (3) a strategy for reaching the reader, and (4) a clear message that ties them together, all your efforts will be no more than a wrestling match with words that results in an ugly document.

Write on a Stable Foundation

Thorough planning is hard work, but it makes writing easier and more enjoyable because it provides structure and direction which keep you on track as you write. As seen in the image below, the idea is that a well-planned foundation keeps your document stable, balanced, forward moving, and unified.

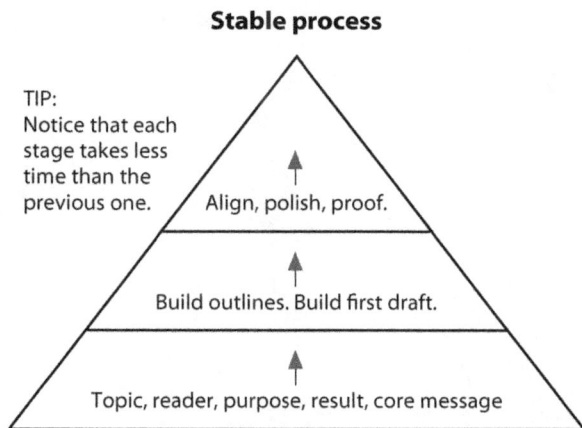

Stable process

TIP:
Notice that each stage takes less time than the previous one.

Align, polish, proof.

Build outlines. Build first draft.

Topic, reader, purpose, result, core message

Building a on a strong foundation and staying on track are two things that many writers, despite their best intentions, often lack, and it causes two problems: it makes your process overly burdensome, which in turn muddies whatever message you are trying to deliver.

✪ Stable planning does more than help you deliver your message. It helps the reader receive it. The better your information is assembled and packaged, the easier it is for the reader to unpack.

Outline in Stages

*You cannot construct unless you get at
the principles of construction.*
Robert Henri

Once you have a foundation in place (the bow-and-arrow tool), you are ready to assemble your outline on top of it.

Keep in mind that a strategic outline is more than a list of contents for the reader. It is a compass that guides you as you write. An outline not only supports your core message, it 'tells' you what to write and it keeps you aligned with your foundation as you go.

Knowing what to write and where to go next are invaluable assets for a writer. But most writers do not use outlines this way. Instead, they make three mistakes that you want to avoid:

- **Do not limit your outline to a list of topics**. When your outline is just a list, it lacks framework. There is no structure to build your document on and around as you write.

- **Do not abandon your outline once writing begins**. When you abandon an outline, you jettison your original strategy, direction, and purpose.

- **Do not get locked into your outline**. Outlining is meant to be a tool, not a straight-jacket. You want a clear framework, but it should serve as a guide. It should not restrict your writing.

Start With a Simple Sketch

The key to outlining is to keep it simple and gradually expand your thinking step-by-step. No matter how complex your document is, always start with a simple sketch—commonly known as a mind map.

Write your core message at the center of a large circle, then place main ideas (high-level topics) around it. Add outer circles for subtopics, related ideas, and examples.

Initial sketch

Your goals with the sketch outline:

- Gather and sort ideas in *simple* form.

- Define and visualize the *scope* of your subject.

- Keep your thinking flexible and *nonlinear.*

- See how ideas *relate* to each other.

- *Experiment* with organization.

A sketch is for brainstorming. You are not concerned about writing yet. You are trying to gather key points, spread them out, and explore connections between them. Don't rush this process. Don't feel that you have to draw conclusions about the content.

You also don't want to be satisfied with too simple of a diagram—just a few circles. You should exhaust this tool during the early stages of planning. Put as much as you can into it and squeeze as much as you can out of it.

Think of the sketch as your blueprint. Several hours—even several days—devoted to a full sketch can be time well spent at the beginning of a project. You will make discoveries, see gaps, raise questions, and, above all, gain command of your message and its many parts.

Ask for feedback early in the process

Solicit as much feedback as you can about your sketch from peers, bosses, and clients. Ask them to make suggestions about content and organization. Let them validate or invalidate your content *and* strategy. All this preparation will pay off tenfold because you will know exactly what you want to say before you move on to a formal outline.

✪ Only when you have a solid initial sketch that you *feel confident about* should you start to transfer it to a formal outline.

Planning and writing require different hats

Planning and then building a document require different kinds of thinking and writing. The first is architectural. The second is construction. Just as architects don't usually *build* buildings, and just as builders don't usually *design* buildings, so you need to wear two different hats when you work.

✪ One of the most common mistakes that writers make is rushing through the outline process, partly because their vision is vague, and partly because they want to avoid the expenditure of time and thinking it requires.

✪ Consider wearing a different hat or shirt, or working in different office spaces, when you perform these two roles. Keep your mindset focused on each one, and don't let them overlap. Why? Because they each require a distinct kind of creativity and thought. Whatever type of writing you are doing, try to approach your planning and outlining with a fluid, flexible, expansive mindset. When you switch hats to actually write, you want to switch gears to a mindset of focused engineering and crisp execution *in alignment with* your plan and core message.

Convert to a Full Outline

With a complete sketch in hand, you are ready to transpose to a full (traditional) outline. But be careful. As mentioned earlier, many people think of a full outline as simply a list of contents for the reader. It is much more than that. It is first and foremost a tool for you as the writer.

✪ The purpose of an outline is to help you transition from blueprint to building. If you design your outline well, it will guide you *as you write.*

Three Kinds of Outlines

Starting with a formal outline can feel rigid, but if you come to it from a well developed sketch, it offers itself as the next logical step of organization.

Three general types of outlines are shown on the following pages. Each has benefits that are applicable to the type and length of document you are assembling.

- Roman numeral outline

- Decimal outline

- Column outline

As you transition from your sketch to an outline, use the type that best suits your project and preferences.

The Roman Numeral Outline

The most traditional outline is a roman numeral format that shows the hierarchy of sections and subsections. This outline is formal, clear, and elegant, so it is well suited to academic, legal, and professional documents.

The roman numeral format is also best for documents that require three or four (no more than six) levels of hierarchy. More than six levels makes things too confusing for you and for the reader. It also creates a formatting headache.

✪ A good way to develop a roman numeral outline is to start with three levels (I-A-1 or 1-1.1-1.1.1). This keeps your structure simple. Once you feel that the overall structure is clear, come back and add or insert more levels of hierarchy as needed.

Roman numeral outline

I. Heading

A. Subheading

　　1. Paragraph heading

　　2. Paragraph heading

　　3. Paragraph heading

B. Subheading

II. Heading

A. Subheading

　　1. Paragraph heading

　　2. Paragraph heading

　　3. Paragraph heading

B. Subheading

III. Heading

A. Subheading

　　1. Paragraph heading

　　2. Paragraph heading

　　3. Paragraph heading

B. Subheading

The Decimal Outline

The decimal outline is a numerical alternative to the roman numeral outline. Because the decimal format is numerically exact, it is easily broken down into 10 or more levels of hierarchy that remain clear for you and for the reader (although 4 levels is the most manageable limit for legible, easy-to-use formatting).

✪ Precision makes the decimal outline the right choice for scientific and technical documents, especially when detailed information needs to be referenced accurately and found quickly.

This outline has developed a reputation for being rigid, impersonal, and military-like. But in its place it works extremely well. The question is always: what will best serve the needs of your ideal reader?

As with the roman numeral outline, don't start here. Develop a sketch first, then convert it to this form for detailed organization.

Decimal outline

1.0 Heading

    1.1 Subheading

        1.1.1 Paragraph heading

        1.1.2 Paragraph heading

        1.1.3 Paragraph heading

    1.2 Subheading

2.0 Heading

    2.1 Subheading

        2.1.1 Paragraph heading

        2.1.2 Paragraph heading

        2.1.3 Paragraph heading

    2.2 Subheading

3.0 Heading

    3.1 Subheading

        3.1.1 Paragraph heading

        3.1.2 Paragraph heading

        3.1.3 Paragraph heading

    3.2 Subheading

The Column Outline

The column outline is an alternative to both the roman numeral and the decimal outlines. It does away with letters and numbers and focuses strictly on organization by subject matter.

✪ One advantage of this outline is that it can be assembled on paper or index cards for easy shuffling.

The column outline also lets you write in any order. For instance, you can begin with a topic in the front, middle, or end of your document and work on any section or subsection at any time. Teams can also divide up the writing once the topic, purpose, and organization have been decided.

Another advantage of the column outline is that it presents a clear image of your whole document. It is easy to get lost once you start writing; the column outline helps you stay focused on the big picture.

The column outline also provides building blocks that you can assemble piece by piece until the whole is finished. The pieces can be worked on independently (by one writer or a team of writers) and continuously reorganized throughout a project. This flexibility can be very useful, especially for long or complex documents.

✪ Keep in mind that you can start with a sketch outline, convert it to a column outline, *then* convert it to roman numeral or decimal format.

Column outline

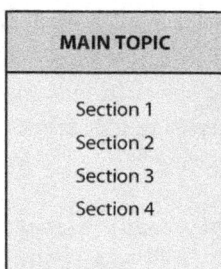

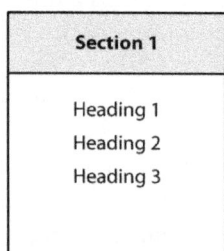

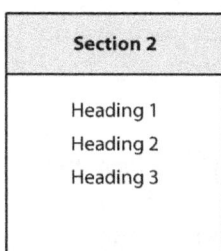

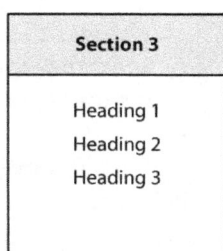

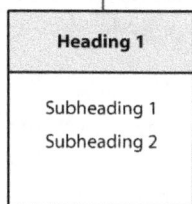

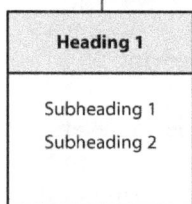

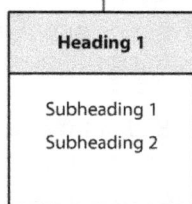

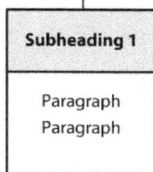

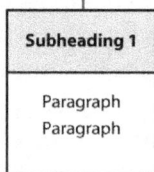

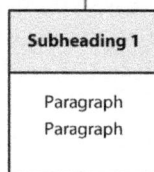

MAIN TOPIC
Section 1
Section 2
Section 3
Section 4

Section 1	Section 2	Section 3
Heading 1	Heading 1	Heading 1
Heading 2	Heading 2	Heading 2
Heading 3	Heading 3	Heading 3

Heading 1	Heading 1	Heading 1
Subheading 1	Subheading 1	Subheading 1
Subheading 2	Subheading 2	Subheading 2

Subheading 1	Subheading 1	Subheading 1
Paragraph	Paragraph	Paragraph
Paragraph	Paragraph	Paragraph

How to Expand an Outline

An effective to build a document is to start with a sketch and then expand it through seven steps of outlining and writing. 'Expanding' an outline is more than a method of planning. It is a way to engineer and control your document in precise stages.

Documents are not usually managed this way because most people do not follow a writing plan. They draft a quick outline and start writing. Sentences turn into paragraphs and then into sections, but because the structure is weak the document gets loosely *written* rather than strategically *built.*

Expanded outlines produce the opposite effect. They help you determine everything ahead of time—content, organization, purpose, and strategy—so that you can assemble the pieces around your core message. This allows you to follow a writing plan the way a general contractor follows a blueprint.

Expanding an outline in seven steps may seem extreme at first. But as you practice this discipline, you will discover that it makes writing easier. Why? Because it relieves you of always having to bear the burden of the entire document. Instead, you rely on your plan and just focus on each current stage of the process.

Below is a brief description of each stage, with a summary diagram to help you see all of them as part of one larger process.

1. **Sketch**. See previous details above about creating an initial sketch outline—*after* you develop the bow-and-arrow and before assembling a formal outline.

2. **Topics**. Full outlines (roman numeral, decimal, column) tend to be written in passive voice because the topics are not saying anything to anyone. They are just a list, and writing them as just a list is an easy first step.

3. **Tasks**. To sharpen your outline, rewrite the topics in active voice so that each one becomes an instruction *to yourself* about what to write. This adjustment will give you direction and add crispness to your text.

4. **Section summaries**. A section summary is a high-level explanation of what the section will convey: the message behind the contents. Formulating a summary can provide a guideline and borders to keep you aligned with your message as you expand each section.

   ✪ Show your section summaries to clients, managers, team members, and stakeholders to get their feedback *before* you start writing full sections. Doing so can bring unexpected focus to your document.

5. **Paragraph briefs**. The purpose of a paragraph brief is to pinpoint the theme of the paragraph before you write it. A paragraph brief does not *explain* the theme; it states the skeleton idea. The goal is to grasp that idea for yourself, not finalize its expression for the reader. You will do that later when you develop the first draft.

6. **Sentence statements**. Write short bullets of main ideas that can be expanded later into full sentences. These are your individual building blocks. You will expand them and join them together later.

7. **Table of contents**. Convert your task outline back to a list of topics. Only now does your outline become a reference tool for the reader. (You will be surprised how much your original outline has changed for the better.)

7 stages of an outline

1	Sketch	Gather ideas loosely in an experimental wheel around the core message. Draw lines to show relationships between ideas. Keep your thinking informal and flexible.
2	Topics	Organize sketch ideas into a structured outline. List topics in passive voice. (Example: "Expanded outlines")
3	Tasks	Rewrite topics in active voice, as tasks that 'tell' you what to write. (Example: "Explain how to expand outlines")
4	Section Summaries	Write one or two short paragraphs that explain the message of each major section. Keep these summaries nearby for reference as you write.
5	Paragraph Briefs	Write one sentence to convey the central message of each intended paragraph.
6	Sentence Statements	Write short phrases (or bullets) for each point you intend to make in a paragraph. Build a complete skeleton of the first draft that focuses strictly on content. Then merge sentences into paragraphs and polish them for clarity.
7	Table of Contents	Rewrite the tasks from step 3 as a table of contents. Do this as a last step before preparing the final draft.

The Table Outline

Another way to develop an outline is to build a table to include all the elements of your topic and all the sections of your outline which can be done easily in MS Word.

✪ A table outline lets you see your whole plan at once and lets you outline and write *at the same time.*

Using a table outline, you can quickly move sections of text around (and even hide some columns while working on others).

Team members and clients will like this tool because they can review your work electronically, mark changes, add content, and make comments—all before you create the first draft. Meanwhile, you can experiment with organization without worrying about page formatting or writing style.

Another advantage of the table outline is that it can combine content from your bow-and-arrow, your sketch outline, and your full outline to show the complete picture of your document strategy. It lets you have everything in one place for easy reference as you build sections and paragraphs.

✪ The table outline is a flexible tool that you can adapt to any project. It is also a helpful tool to give to subject-matter experts who need to supply you with key content.

✪ Adapt the table outline to your purpose by including more columns. Having a 'comments' column, for example, can be useful for adding notes and getting feedback.

Example of a table outline

Topic				
Reader				
Purpose				
Result				
Core Message				

Topic	Task	Main ideas	Expanded
passive voice	active voice	• idea • idea	Expand each bullet idea into sentences and/or paragraphs
table outlines	Explain the benefits of a table outline	• See everything at once. • Outline and write at the same time • Move sections easily	A table outline not only lets you see your whole document plan at once. It enables you to outline and write at the same time, or as you see the need for either. A table outline also lets you move sections of text around quickly and easily. It is a very flexible and adaptable tool.

Build in Stages Around Your Core Message

The preparatory stages of bow-and-arrow, sketch, and outlining are designed to give a comprehensive framework for building strategic content in stages around your core message.

Your core message is more than a comprehensive statement. It becomes the central rod running through your entire document and tying all the pieces together. With the core as your center, you can introduce and roll out each major theme to the reader, explaining how they relate to the core. This can weave a clear, concise, complete message in easy-to-digest form.

Wrap thematic content around the core

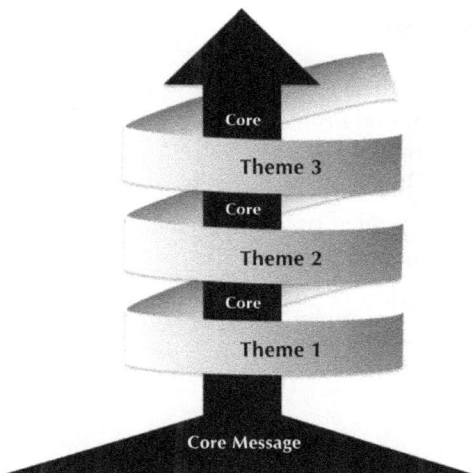

✪ As you introduce themes and build them into your document, don't stray from the core message. You want to give your reader a solid handle to rely on as you introduce new themes and related ideas—all of which should tie into and echo your core message.

Your Core Message is not a Thesis Statement

A thesis statement appears at the beginning of an essay. Its purpose is to introduce your topic, make a clear statement about the topic, and summarize how the topic will unfold in the upcoming essay or section.

The word 'thesis' comes from a Latin musical term which means 'downbeat' — loosely, 'setting the tone' for a piece of writing, the author's premise or main point of view or argument.

Your thesis may be connected to your core message; it may point to your core message; but it is *not* the same as your core message.

✪ Whereas a thesis is *stated* in written form, your core message should be *implied* throughout your document.

✪ Defining the core message is an exercise for you as the writer. You need not tell the reader what it is. Rather your entire document should be a reflection and embodiment of it.

Sharpen Your Message

Grasp the subject and the words will come.
Cato

What the Reader Wants

Readers do not want to be confused, manipulated, or led astray. They want access to the story or information (the core message) behind your words, and usually in as few words as possible. Here are a few other things that most readers want:

- **Ease of use**. Readers do not mind having to work, but the material must be easy to manage. Keep your direction obvious and your message clear.

- **Control**. Readers do not want to fight for control. Give them a quick handle on your message.

- **Noninterference**. The modern reader wants reading to be convenient, fast, and pain free. The best solution for all of these is simplicity and clarity. Get to the point.

- **Results**. Readers want to be informed, instructed, inspired, or entertained. Know which result you are trying to achieve.

- **Good examples**. Don't expect readers to know what you are trying to say. Give crisp examples. Examples strengthen your writing and reinforce your message.

- **Invisible author**. Readers usually do not want to know about you. Keep yourself in the background as much as possible.

The Writer's Job

Your job is (always) to make the reader's job easier. When a document is disorganized, directionless, and unfocused, readers have to struggle. If you are wrestling as you write, you can be sure readers will have to wrestle as they read.

Reaching the reader is your goal. Knowing the reader helps you grasp your message, aim it, and deliver it. To help the reader, however, you must be certain about the message in your own mind first.

If you are not helping the reader—if your ideas are ambiguous, your sentences fuzzy, and your direction uncertain—it is because you are unsure of your message. Go back to the planning stage. Analyze the topic more thoroughly. Plan a strategy. Build your outline step by step.

✪ Remember: you are always writing for the benefit of the reader according to your strategy toward a specific outcome.

The Writer's Limitations

The average writer has limitations that even experienced writers must work to avoid:

- **Lack of purpose and strategy**. Surprisingly, many writers never define what they want to achieve when writing. They have a vague feeling yet cannot articulate it. They cannot pinpoint a strategic target or intended result. If you can, you are a step ahead.

- **Foggy concept**. A good idea is not a core message. Do not guess. Be definite about what you want to say and why. If you are not sure, it means it is not time to start writing. Keep distilling the core message. Be certain beforehand so you can be clear when you start writing.

- **Poor planning**. Even when your core message is clear, a disorganized delivery will leave the reader frustrated. This is often a sign that you drafted a brief outline without formulating a strategy for presenting it. Remember that a good outline is a tool for you as the writer. Use it to make your job easier.

- **Haste**. Most people do not allow sufficient time for working out their ideas *before* writing. They skip planning and jump into writing, assuming that a document will work itself out as they write. Don't make this mistake. Discipline yourself. Appreciate the creative aspects of analyzing, planning, and organizing your message before trying to deliver it.

- **Editing while writing**. Editing while writing is a misuse of time and energy. It is also a symptom of poor planning. If you do not organize your topic, strategy, and core message in advance, you will keep fiddling with sentence structure as you write. Writing will quickly become rewriting and editing will become nothing more than frustrating repair work.

- **Writer's block**. In most cases, writer's block means 'idea' block or 'planning' block. It has nothing to do with writing or your writing ability. Either your concept is murky and cannot be formulated as a clear message, or you are stuck with no direction. If you find yourself in this position, go back to the planning stage or accept that you have to start over. Never place blame on your lack of ability or creativity.

The Reader's Limitations

Even when you know your message and have a good strategy, remember that the reader also has limitations. Keep these in mind as you write.

- **Attention**. Readers have a short attention span. To stay alert, they need a frequent pause (paragraph break), reminder (connecting idea), or boost (new or exciting idea). Use these three devices and you will hold the reader on the page.

- **Quantity**. Readers prefer small bites and time to chew, especially when information is complex or new. Limit the amount of information in each paragraph. Assume the reader is seeing it for the first time.

- **Sequence**. The mind receives information best when ideas are presented in logical sequence. If the sequence is mixed up, the reader will be, too. Proper sequence is crucial to delivering your message well.

- **Connections**. If the relationship between the whole (core message) and parts (related ideas) is not clear, the document will fall apart. It needs this connective tissue to keep it together. Are you introducing the whole and explaining how parts fit into it; or are you introducing details and explaining how they connect to form a whole? Make your approach clear so the reader can make connections easily.

- **Visualization**. Each reader's mind works differently, but everyone achieves clarity when an idea can be visualized in three dimensions. This is when an idea comes alive. Give the reader a solid handle on your message by using vivid analogies and concrete examples.

- **Subjectivity**. The reader does not necessarily think or feel the way you do. Your task is to bend your writing to the reader's point of view or else persuade the reader to look through your lens. In both cases the goal is to accommodate the reader.

Writing and Rewriting

Writing, rewriting, and editing are separate steps with different purposes. Try not to mix them or do them at the same time. Otherwise you will weaken the fabric of your communication. If you find yourself editing too much, or if you find yourself editing and rewriting at the same time, it means your core message or outline—or both—are unclear. Instead of laying content on top of a well conceived foundation, you are wrestling with words. Go back to your sketch or bow-and-arrow. Get realigned with the core.

Writing includes section summaries and paragraph briefs. The purpose of these stages of initial writing is to lay ideas on top of your outline. The purpose is not to finalize the wording (*how* something is said). The purpose is to pin down the core message (*what* is being said). The more you focus on *exactly* what you want to say, the better you will be able to say it. When you write strong briefs, it becomes much easier to expand them into complete paragraphs and full sections.

The goal of rewriting is to improve the organization of ideas and clarify what is muddy. Rewriting does not mean starting over. It means adjusting sentences so they align with the core message of their paragraph. Sometimes rewriting is as simple as converting passive voice into active voice for crispness. Converting to active voice will also reveal where your writing is vague and 'soft'.

The goal of editing is to sharpen and polish your final expression. Editing should not be an extension of writing or rewriting. It should stand alone as a top coat, a touch up, a refinement. Good editing is finesse.

Three Levels of Editing

Editing can be done on three levels—each at different times. Know which level you are doing in the moment and concentrate with a mindset suited to that task.

Comprehensive editing deals with the organization of a whole document or section. Is there a unified core message that ties everything together? Is the presentation of ideas sequential and understandable? Can the large pieces be reorganized to better deliver the message to the reader? Ideally, all these questions are resolved before, not after, writing. Nevertheless, sometimes a comprehensive editor—who is often the writer—needs to examine an already written document, not for its sentence structure or style, but for its overall comprehension.

Copy editing looks at paragraph structure and sentence clarity. Do paragraphs convey a central idea? Do they flow well? Are sentences well connected and clear? Is the reader being kept on track? Copy editing is not rewriting. It is a process of making adjustments to the structure of paragraphs and sentences.

Proof editing is a check of spelling, punctuation, cross references, and footnotes—the final, physical details of a document. It is a search with a microscope. It assumes that strategy, structure, and clarity have been taken care of, so it does not focus on them at all—which is why a final proof edit should be fairly quick and painless.

Build Strong Paragraphs and Sentences

Paragraphs. Strive to limit each paragraph to one idea or thought. Make things easy for the reader. Introduce an idea, elucidate its main points, and then conclude or connect to a new idea in a new paragraph.

Visually, a paragraph tells the reader that a new idea is coming. Most readers subconsciously assess the demands of an upcoming paragraph by its length. That is the only thing they have to go by before reading. Short paragraphs make it possible for readers to keep plunging ahead.

It is hard work to write short, clear paragraphs. You have to pinpoint each idea and streamline your explanation. You have to find the simplest way to introduce a thought, develop it, and wrap it up (or link it to the next paragraph). These demands, however, strengthen your writing and enable more comprehensive reading.

Don't worry about threading each paragraph to the next one, and don't try to explain everything about each idea. Say something as clearly as you can, then move on. And don't be afraid to break a long or complex idea into two or more paragraphs.

✪ Remember that paragraphs are packages for delivering a clear message to the reader. Make them easy to unwrap by getting to the point quickly.

Sentences. The best way to build strong sentences is to keep them short. Short sentences, like short paragraphs, are good for the reader and the writer.

The art of writing sentences is to link phrases together ("syntax"—to tie together) so they interlace in the reader's mind. There is no perfect way to do this, but one approach is to use simple phrases and simple sentences.

Musicians learn by mastering notes, then phrases, then long passages until they can tie everything together in a unified piece of music. Go slowly. Strive for clarity in each phrase, then each sentence, then each paragraph. This will unify your message and reveal a style that is already yours.

The finest musicians also go a step further. While mastering the notes and phrases of a piece of music, they try to comprehend the piece as a whole. What was the composer's intention? What were the circumstances in which the piece was conceived and written? What effect is the work meant to have on the listener? Understanding all these things and keeping them in mind while performing a piece adds a unified dimension to the work that a mere repetition of notes can never achieve. The same is true of a piece of writing whose core message is clearly understood and conveyed *as a whole* by the writer.

Remember that simple phrases and short sentences are a technique. They don't automatically make you a good writer. They may even make you feel like a worse writer at first because all the fat and fun seem gone. Push past this point. Let brevity show you the beauty of strong, clear sentences.

✪ Be specific. Be definite. Say what you mean without over-explaining it. Do not qualify your statements. State ideas in positive, not negative, form.

Verbs, Nouns, Adjectives, and Adverbs

The best way to put sentences together is to strip them down to the bare bones of writing and reveal ideas in their simplest form. To do this, practice writing without adjectives and adverbs. You will be surprised how unnecessary adjectives and adverbs usually are, and how powerful your writing can be without them.

Go slowly. Add adjectives for color. Add adverbs for emphasis. Never let an adjective or adverb do the work of a noun or verb.

Think of nouns and verbs as the platform for each idea. Add adjectives for support and adverbs for reinforcement, but don't let either of them distract the reader from your message.

One way to control adjectives and adverbs is to limit them to one per sentence, and to prune whenever possible.

Example of too many adjectives and adverbs:

Writing is a very simple process once you really know how to write well. You gather good concepts, compose them as organized ideas, then use different words to precisely construct cogent sentences and to build fluid, connected paragraphs.

Example of minimizing adjectives and adverbs:

Writing is a simple process once you know how to write. You

gather concepts, compose them as ideas, then use words to construct sentences and build paragraphs.

Active and Passive Voice

Use the active voice as much as possible. You will, by necessity, weave passive-voice sentences into some paragraphs, and this is good for contrast, but never let the passive voice outweigh the active. The reason is vitality. The active voice is bright, lively, and immediate. It stands ideas up on their feet. It gets the reader's attention and holds interest. The passive voice, by contrast, is sluggish and indirect. It makes the reader work too hard to unravel sentences and get at their meaning.

The passive voice feels easy to use because it lets you string ideas out as abstract concepts and terms, without crispness. The active voice makes you think and be definite, whereas the passive voice *allows* you to be vague (which is why passive-voice sentences are hard to understand).

Be vigilant about adopting the active voice. Otherwise you are sure to slip into passive voice and lose the reader.

✪ Converting passive-voice sentences to active voice is an excellent way to freshen your message.

From Passive to Active Voice

Example of passive voice with adjectives and adverbs:

The process of acquiring locations to build a cellular network is a critical element in the successful and timely deployment of the system. Americana has extensive experience around the world in locating and acquiring the optimal properties for placement of the antennas and accompanying equipment for base stations. In addition, preparation has been done to identify and adapt past learnings to the Brazilian environment. This process has been initiated by Americana already in São Paulo and Rio de Janeiro. This effort has involved hiring appropriate local experts to expedite the potentially lengthy site acquisition process and ultimately meet the rollout plan for the proposed cellular network.

Example of active voice with fewer words:

Acquiring antenna base-station sites is vital to implementing the cellular network. Americana has located and acquired worldwide sites for base stations and has already developed a site-acquisition plan for Brazil. To expedite the potentially long acquisition process and ensure a successful rollout plan, Americana has also begun hiring local experts in São Paulo and Rio de Janeiro.

More Examples of Voice and Person

Passive voice, third-person

The vendor's project plan will be coordinated and executed by the project manager according to the client's specifications.

Active voice, first-person:

ABC's project manager will coordinate and execute the project plan according to XYZ's exact specifications.

Passive voice, third-person:

A test plan will be required to be developed by the vendor and submitted to and approved by the project manager. In addition, unit and system testing will be performed before user acceptance testing.

Active voice, third-person:

The vendor will be required to develop a test plan and submit it to the project manager for approval. The vendor will also need to perform unit and system testing prior to user acceptance testing.

✪ Passive-voice reveals information indirectly. Active-voice states facts directly.

Grammar, Punctuation, and Spelling

Grammar is the formal construction of words into phrases. The rules of grammar, however, are not laws that must be followed under all circumstances, so try not to be afraid of them.

✪ Many people learn grammar as a system of writing rules that they are afraid to break, without realizing that these rules exist to *help* deliver a clear message.

Make your message the priority and let the rules of grammar support it. Think of rules as bridges that help ideas cross the gap between you and the reader. Use grammar to send your message across.

Punctuation (to 'puncture') is the organization of word flow and emphasis. Punctuation marks are symbols that tell the reader where to start, where to pause (and for how long), what to connect, how to connect, and when to stop.

Treat punctuation like grammar: as a set of *guidelines* for sending a clear message. Use punctuation to give directions to the reader, and use it sparingly. Don't let punctuation clutter or obstruct your message.

Spelling is the organization of words into letters. More importantly, it is the division of words into prefixes, suffixes, and roots—the sediment of language. Roll up your sleeves as you write and dig your hands in this rich soil. Take time to search for the buried gems of etymology. Don't worry about how words are spelled. Instead, learn how they are constructed. Study prefixes, suffixes, and roots. This is a never-ending education and in most cases spelling will follow from it naturally and enjoyably.

Understanding Words

The more you understand etymology, the more definite your writing will become. Your choice of language will be more exact. Your expression of ideas will be more succinct. Your writing will be more satisfying for you and for the reader.

Examples of Word Construction

The root 'pathos' (feeling)

- sym-pathy (with feeling)

- em-pathy (feeling for)

- a-pathy (without feeling)

- anti-pathy (against feeling)

The prefix 'para' (next to)

- para-llel (next to another)

- para-graph (next to written)

- para-medic (next to a doctor)

- para-site (next to food)

The root 'plicate' (to fold)

- com-plicate (fold together)

- du-plicate (two fold, double)

- im-plicate (fold, or twist, in)

- ex-plicate (unfold, explain)

Go for Great Design

Work always as if you were a master.
Expect from yourself a masterpiece.
Robert Henri

The Goal of Page Design

The goal of page design is to help you deliver your message visually, which is usually enhanced when the reader sees the following:

* Generous margins and white space.

* Text that is easy to read.

* Consistent, uncluttered formatting.

* Headings that stand out.

* Clear tables and graphics.

When the visual message of a page is unorganized and unpleasant to look at, it becomes a barrier—an obstacle course— that the reader has to struggle through to find the message. The same thing happens when a page is over-designed with too many fonts and sizes of fonts, with too many colors and graphics, or with graphics that dominate instead of support the message.

Too much or not enough emphasis on page design distracts the reader and blurs your message. Therefore, build your page design with care.

✪ When it comes to page design, strive for simplicity and visual clarity around a single, central message.

Techniques for Page Design

Strong page design echoes the message of your text or idea. So the first thing to be clear about is the message: its content, its purpose, its tone.

Do you want your message to sound and look professional, technical, instructive, elegant, entertaining, shocking? Be definite about the effect you want to achieve, then build a design to reinforce that. Try not to get lost in design techniques. Focus on your message and its intended result.

The best way to stay focused is to keep page design simple. It is easier to add design elements than it is to remove them, so go slowly. Include a design element only when you are certain why you need to include it. Start with some basic ingredients of good design:

- **White space**. Let the page breathe. Use generous margins, ample leading (line spacing), and liberal space between sections. Simple page elements look nice and convey confidence, both of which relax the reader.

- **Power points**. It has been shown that the page (for English readers) has two 'power' points: the top-left corner and the lower-right corner. If you want to draw the reader's visual attention, do so in these two spots.

- **Fonts**. In most cases, use one or two fonts. Use one for headings, another for body text. This creates contrast and visually separates different kinds of information.

- **Font sizes**. Software programs usually default to even-sized fonts, so most people select either 10- or 12-point for their body text. But 11-point is, in many cases, the most legible size. The difference is subtle but it has an important effect on the reader.

  Font designs also vary, so do not rely on one point size as a standard. Use your eye. Think of the reader.

- **Tables**. Tables are a superb tool for conveying messages because they break information into comprehensible pieces. It is easy, however, for tables to get in their own way—for example, when they are too boxy, when the lines are too thick, when the text looks cramped, and when headings are hard to read. All of these visual miscues turn the reader off and obscure the message *inside* a table.

Simple Style Sheets

Styles are a great tool, but they give the average user more options than he or she needs. And the default styles of many software programs are not up to professional writing standards.

The best remedy is to use as few styles as possible. In most cases you will need only the following:

- 1 header

- 1 footer

- 4 or 5 levels of headings

- 1 body text

- 1 bullet style

- 1 number style

- 1 note style

Create the styles you need and delete as many of the other default styles as you can. A shorter scrolling list of styles makes it easier to assign styles and to change style attributes as you write. It will also keep you focused on your main purpose: delivering a clear message to the reader.

As with design elements, don't create extra styles until you are sure you need them. It is easy to get overburdened by having to update and keep track of styles.

✪ Keep style names short and in *formatting* order.

Copying Text From Other Documents

Business documents are frequently cobbled together from other documents instead of written from scratch. Whole sections are usually copied and pasted. Although this is understandable, it is not an excuse for sloppy writing. When you copy text from other documents, follow these guidelines to ensure freshness:

- **Do not copy styles along with the text**. With some software programs, whenever you copy and paste text from other documents you bring the styles with it. This can foul up your style names, change your style settings, and add extra styles that you don't want.

  ✪ When pasting text from other documents, use the "paste special" option; select 'paste as unformatted text'. Then reformat with your styles.

- **Reverse-outline and rewrite**. When pasting text from other documents, always reverse-engineer it. Analyze each section of pasted text from the point of view of subject, purpose, intended result, and message. Does it coincide with the proposal strategy? Is it a smooth fit? If not, rewrite the text to make it seamless.

- **Adjust person and voice**. Go through all pasted text and edit it into consistent voice and person. Remember that the weakest form of writing is passive voice, third-person. The active voice is more telling. It sends a more swift and compelling message.

Standards for Text

Text affects the reader in subtle ways, so be deliberate. Be sure that your text helps and does not hinder the reader.

- **Make headings stand out**. Headings are pointers for the reader. Make them distinct without letting them overwhelm the body text. To achieve contrast, set headings in bold and either in a different font (such as a sans-serif font) or in a larger size than your body text. Be sure there is adequate white space above headlines to set them apart from the preceding paragraph, and enough white space below so that they float gently above their companion text.

- **Avoid arbitrary capitalization**. Follow general rules of capitalization. Do not arbitrarily capitalize words, or at least do it sparingly. Too much capitalization makes the page busy and distracts the reader.

- **Use italics for emphasis**. If you want to emphasize words, put them in italics, not in uppercase (all capital) letters. Words in uppercase are hard to read, especially when there are many uppercase words in a row. Never put an entire paragraph in uppercase. It is simply too hard to read.

WORDS PRINTED IN UPPERCASE DOMINATE THE PAGE AND ARE VISUALLY PAINFUL TO READ, ESPECIALLY WHEN THERE ARE SEVERAL UPPERCASE WORDS IN A ROW. NEVER PUT AN ENTIRE PARAGRAPH IN UPPERCASE.

- **Use serif fonts for body text**. Use a serif font (one with curls, like Book Antiqua) for body text. It makes reading easier and comprehension faster. Sans-serif fonts (the ones *without curls,* like Arial) are designed for headings, notes, and captions, but are hard to read in long lines and long paragraphs.

- **Do not underline words**. Underlining is a holdover from typewriter days when bold and italic were not available. Use bold or italic instead. Most software programs include an underlining feature, but they place the underline too close to the bottom of letters, which muddies the text and interferes with reading.

- Do not underline text. Underlining fuzzies the text, 'scratches' the page, and interferes with reading.

- **Type only one space after each period**. Professional typesetters use one space after the period. Two spaces is amateurish. Using two spaces also creates gaps which break the visual continuity of a paragraph.

- **Avoid small type**. Small type makes the reader's job harder. As a standard, use 11-point text or larger for body text. Avoid type that is smaller than 10-point, especially for long paragraphs.

- **Use justified text**. Ragged text makes the reader strain subconsciously. Justified text is visually neater. It also makes reading easier because the eye is able to jump from the same point at the end of each line to reach the beginning of the next line.

- **Manage space between paragraphs**. Use one carriage return (hit the return key once, not twice) to create space between paragraphs. Adjust the paragraph space-before and space-after settings in your software program. A nice standard is to make the space-after approximately two-thirds of your line spacing (called leading). For example, if your leading is 15-point, set the space-after at 10-point. Most importantly, use your eye. Don't just insert a gap in the page. Adjust the space for the reader's ease of use.

- **Manage the space between letters**. For the most part, leave the space between letters and words alone. Avoid the habit of stretching words by increasing the space between letters (like this):

O R G A N I Z E D   D O C U M E N T

Stretching words in normal sentences is unnatural and unpleasant to the eye. Use bold type or a larger font instead. Reserve stretched text as a design technique for cover titles, posters, and other marketing material.

Standards for Graphics

Try to make all the graphics in your document consistent in size, appearance, and placement. Determine one size and color scheme. Place each graphic in the same location on its page (such as flush left). The reader will subconsciously thank you for making different graphics available in the same way.

Modern software creates the false sense that graphics will take care of themselves; that they do not need careful handling. Don't let this fool you. Keep your reader in mind. Make graphics simple, consistent, and elegant.

Document development often involves importing graphics from other documents. The result is a hodge-podge of images with no visual consistency. Because the graphics were designed for other documents, they tend to stand alone rather than complement each other and the text. They may also vary in size, shape, color, fonts, and format, so the reader has to reorient to each new graphic.

Suggestions For Graphics

- **Adjust size**. When importing graphics from other documents, adjust their size and width to standard proportions. Make sure they stay inside the margins.

- **Adjust placement**. Place (hang) graphics from the top left corner—where the paragraph would normally begin. Center graphics on a page only if the text headings are also centered. In other words, be sure that the graphics complement the page design and format.

- **Adjust fonts**. Whenever possible, change the fonts in graphics to match the fonts in your document. An attractive standard is to use the same font that you use in headings and tables.

- **Create consistent headings**. Graphics often include their own headings or titles. Delete those headings or crop them so they cannot be seen, then substitute a heading style from your document's style sheet. Giving them consistent headings will link them in the reader's mind and create visual unity throughout the document.

- **Adjust colors or convert to gray scale**. As a general rule, if the color design of your document is black and white, convert all graphics to gray scale. This creates visual uniformity and prevents graphics from competing with the text. Remember that the role of graphics is to support, complement, and facilitate delivery of the core message. A large color graphic in the middle of an otherwise black-and-white document tends to draw undue attention to itself or simply look out of place, neither of which is professional.

- **Avoid heavy borders**. Thick borders squeeze and imprison graphics. They also darken the impression of the page. If you use borders, keep them thin (or reduce their color percentage to less than 80 percent). The goal is for graphics to 'float' on the page and be as non-distracting as possible.

    ✪ Try your images without borders first. This often enhances the image and lightens the page.

Standards for Tables

A table is an excellent communication tool, yet its format can clutter a document and make the reader's task harder. A table defeats its own purpose when it obscures rather than delivers the message inside.

- **Reformat imported tables.** If you import tables from other documents, reformat them to match the table design of your style sheet. You want all tables to have the same look and feel.

- **Use a standard design.** Set up a standard table design that includes delicate lines (1/4-inch thick). The default settings in most word-processing programs are not acceptable for professional design, so take the time to customize your settings.

- **Adjust line spacing.** Be sure text boxes have more space above the text than below it. This helps text rest above the lines rather than float in the boxes, which makes it easier to read. But remember: for this you have to change the default paragraph settings in your software.

- **Make text readable.** A common mistake is to put small text in tight boxes. Avoid this trend. Use a font size that is easy to read. A good minimum size is 9-point. If you must, use 8.5-point. Smaller than that is hard reading for an adult. Remember that the idea behind table design is not to squeeze all your information into it, but to make it easy for the reader to get information out of it. *Readers like spacious, legible tables.*

- **Set headings off from their tables.** Make it easy for

the reader to distinguish between a table heading and table text. Put table headings in bold against a shaded background (15 to 25 percent black), or use white text against a solid background.

- **Make tables transparent**. In general, make tables as transparent and easy to read as possible. All too often, a table obstructs the information in it.

✪ Remember: the important thing is not the table but the information inside. Compare the tables on the next page and notice the difference between:

- Thick borders vs. Thin borders

- Plain headings vs. Contrasted headings

- Floating text vs. Anchored text

- Centered text vs. Flush-left text

- Uppercase letters vs. Lowercase letters

- Centered numbers vs. Right-aligned numbers

- Too many $ signs • Just enough $ signs

Table comparison

CLUMSY AND CLUTTERED

ITEM	CODE	LOCATION	QUANTITY	VALUE
DESKTOP PCS	CPU	HQ1	9	$18,000.00
DESKTOP MONITORS	MON	HQ2	9	$3,000.00
LAPTOPS	LAP	BR1	12	$27,000.00
PRINTERS	PRT	ENT	25	$10,000.00
BACKUP DRIVES	CDR	ENT	10	$3,000.00
TOTAL				$65,000.00

Clean and Clear

Item	Code	Location	Quantity	Value
Desktop Pcs	CPU	HQ1	9	$18,000.00
Desktop Monitors	MON	HQ2	9	$3,000.00
Laptops	LAP	BR1	12	$27,000.00
Printers	PRT	ENT	25	$10,000.00
Backup Drives	CDR	ENT	10	$3,000.00
Total				**$65,000.00**

Professional and Elegant

Item	Code	Location	Quantity	$ Value
Desktop Pcs	CPU	HQ1	9	18,000.00
Desktop Monitors	MON	HQ2	9	3,000.00
Laptops	LAP	BR1	12	27,000.00
Printers	PRT	ENT	25	10,000.00
Backup Drives	CDR	ENT	10	3,000.00
				$65,000.00

Learn AIDA

You should drive the reader on to a conclusion.
Robert Henri

The AIDA Method

The AIDA writing method originated as a marketing strategy in advertising and sales, but it can be applied to *any kind of* written material, including memos, letters, and executive summaries. AIDA stands for:

A   **Attention**—grab the reader's *Attention.*

I   **Interest**—generate *Interest.*

D   **Desire**—create *Desire* (or *Decision*) in the reader.

A   **Action**—prompt the reader to take *Action.*

The AIDA method stresses strategy and result, which should be the aim of all your writing. Practice this technique. Use AIDA to build your framework *before* you write a memo or letter or executive summary.

Business Memos and Emails

A memo is more than a short note. It is a crisp message whose purpose is to inform or instruct. As the Latin origin of 'memorandum' implies, a memo is something to be remembered.

AIDA is perfect for this because it helps you organize your message strategically and deliver it with verve. When writing memos or emails with AIDA, build a skeleton of four parts, pinpoint the core message of each part, expand into paragraphs, then polish the whole.

Here is one strategy for building an effective memo or email:

A   **Attention**—Arouse/alert the reader.

I   **Interest**—State the key facts, findings, goals.

D   **Desire**—Convey the impact and consequences.

A   **Action**—List the steps to be taken.

AIDA is effective because it combines your planning, organizing, outlining, and writing in one tool. You control each stage of writing and the whole document at the same time. Most importantly, you manage the message that you want to deliver.

✪ When preparing the sketch for your memo, remember that you can write a list of topics or a set of tasks, or both.

Memo sketch

FROM: Paul Leda, Chief Financial Officer

TO: All Company Officers

RE: Company cars and annual mileage

• State that the cost to drive a company car may be going up.

• Describe how fleet expenses have skyrocketed.

• Explain that a new policy will apply next year.

• Outline a few steps for drivers to follow.

Memo final

FROM: Paul Leda, Chief Financial Officer

TO: All Company Officers

RE: Company cars and annual mileage

Your cost to drive a company car MAY be going up next year—depending on how many miles you drive annually.

In the last 12 months, fleet expenses have skyrocketed. Insurance rates have tripled, maintenance costs have jumped 44 percent, and employee miles have doubled.

To help reduce costs, company mileage next year will be limited to a maximum of 10,000 miles per year. For mileage exceeding 10,000, you will be required to reimburse the company 19 cents per mile (half the federal reimbursement rate).

Please take a few minutes to familiarize yourself with the monthly mileage log (attached) which will be in effect on the first of January. For questions, or if you feel your situation merits an exception to this new policy, please contact Accounting at ext. 22.

Business Letters

A business letter should be formal and informative, with a personal tone that refrains from being casual. Whereas a memo is factual and sent to many people at once, a business letter usually addresses an issue of professional concern between two people.

Here is one strategy for building an effective business letter:

A   **Attention**—Introduce the reason for writing.

I   **Interest**—List/develop the main points.

D   **Desire—Draw** conclusions/Propose alternatives.

A   **Action**—Provide decisions or action steps.

✪ Limit business letters to four paragraphs and to one page. This will maximize the AIDA formula and produce a strong, organized message.

Business letter sketch

RE: catalog printing services

• Reconnect since our previous conversation.

• Outline the project requirements.

• Suggest pricing parameters.

• Request an exact quote.

Business letter final

RE: catalog printing services

Dear Mr. Cannon,

During our strategy meeting this morning, I mentioned to my staff some of the proposals which you and I talked about at the conference. They suggested I give you a few more details about what we need next month.

The catalog will be standard size, with 190 pages and 245 color images. Contrary to what I told you earlier, there will be no page bleeds. We would need 20,000 catalogs by the 10th of the month and another 15,000 by the 20th of the month.

For the last four years we have received discounts from our printer in the form of 20 percent after 5,000 copies and 40 percent after 10,000 copies. We would like to know if you can match or beat these rates, and whether you have any additional proposals or incentives for us.

Although time is short, as it always seems to be in this business, I would appreciate receiving your bottom-line quotes by the 25th of this month so that we can make a decision and still meet our normal delivery schedule.

I look forward to hearing from you.

Sincerely yours,

Executive Summaries

Whether an executive summary is one or twenty pages long, you can approach it the same way you do a letter or memo. The key is to follow the AIDA method and limit your organization to four parts.

Remember that an executive summary is not a report. Its purpose is to provide a succinct overview. To achieve this, stick to main points and include only those details that absolutely must be included to support the main points. An executive summary fails when it digs into content that obscures the main message. Always beware of a summary that starts with big-picture impact and then fizzles into facts.

✪ Don't let an executive summary turn into a report.

Set the subject-matter goals. Limit the scope. Focus on major, executive-level points. If you need to reinforce those points, do so in a follow-up report or proposal.

Here is one AIDA strategy for building an effective summary:

A   **Attention**—Introduce the subject/impact.

I   **Interest**—Explain the background/significance.

D   **Desire**—Describe the *major* findings/costs.

A   **Action**—Outline the *large* solutions/savings.

Limit short *and* long summaries to four sections. Otherwise you will spread your message too thin and lose the reader.

✪ If your summary will exceed two pages, prepare each of the four sections as a list of bullets before writing full paragraphs. Analyze them carefully for message and strategy. This will help you tighten the organization and send a clear message.

AIDA *in Reverse*

You can also approach AIDA *backwards* and start with the call-to-action. What is the final thing that you want the reader to feel or do? This is your purpose for writing so it can be the best place to start your planning so that your communication strategy aligns with it.

A **Action**—what action or result or feeling or imperative do you want to leave the reader with?

D **Desire**—How can you elicit the right want or impulse or motivation?

I **Interest**—How can you generate a deeper interest in what you are trying to promote?

A **Attention**—What is the best object or temptation or point of view that you can use to capture and captivate the reader?

There is a fine line between communication strategy and customer manipulation, but you can see how powerful a simple tool like AIDA can be , and how easy it can bs to use once you master these four steps.

Use AIDA for Web Sites

You can also use the AIDA method to write web pages, especially the home page which is often the most crucial for capturing and convincing the internet reader.

Writing web pages is tricky because you have to write for (1) the search engines that list and rank your web pages and (2) customers who decide—often in seconds—whether to stay and possibly buy from you.

Web pages differ from other kinds of documents in that, instead of telling readers what you want them to hear, you have to answer questions they are silently asking. In AIDA terms, the main questions in their minds are:

A **Attention**—Who are you and what do you provide?

I **Interest**—What can you do specifically for me?

D **Desire**—What will I gain (convenience, benefits, cost)?

A **Action**—How do I proceed (search, respond, buy)?

Although the content and strategy of web pages may differ from standard business documents, you can still plan, organize, and write them the same way. The key is to manage your strategy in four parts (A-I-D-A).

The home page is your front door. Its job is to beckon and open easily. The home page is not meant to be the living room where you entertain guests and make them comfortable. Don't clutter your home page with too much information and too many choices. Use AIDA to establish information priorities and content boundaries for your reader.

✪ Serve the reader. Make information clear. Keep choices simple. Get readers *inside* to where *they want* to go.

Page construction. The internet began as a content (text) based network and all indications are that the internet is clinging to its content-based origins. The clearest evidence comes from search engine companies that use algorithms to find, list, and rank web pages. Those algorithms cannot read graphics and likely never will. They base their analysis solely on the text they find in the source code, particularly on the clarity and richness of your thematic content.

✪ Quality images capture *attention* and create *interest,* but it is from information that internet customers make their *decision* and take *action.*

Because most internet customers are eager for results, build your pages around clear, informative text. Use graphics to highlight and reinforce your *message.*

Page content. Perhaps the most common weakness of web page writing is to write about what your company offers instead of what the reader (the customer) needs. This may seem like a small distinction, but it makes a big difference. The difference is between what your company does and "what it can do for me."

The second weakness of crafting web pages is to write in broad terms and passive voice. Broad language can cover many business bases at once, but it usually defeats its own purpose by diluting—and never delivering—the core message. The passive voice does the same thing by dulling the message and making it hard to get at.

Compare these examples of company descriptions:

Company-focused, vague, and passive:

Providing enterprise-wide IT solutions.

Customer-focused, but still vague and passive:

Customized systems for large financial institutions.

Customer-focused, specific, and active:

We build secure databases for banks and credit unions.

Understand Your Web Strategy

✪ Many if not most web sites *never* tell you what they really do. The images are generic and the content is vague. *It is rare to find a site that gets to the real point.*

✪ There is a strong temptation for companies to jam as much information as possible—every little detail—into their web site, even though customers don't need *and don't want* to know everything.

In the beginning of the internet, content was driven by keywords. As algorithms grew more sophisticated, you could emphasize themes instead of just keywords. As a result, design got more creative, coding got smarter, and sites started looking more slick. But gorgeous pictures and clever coding are not enough. You can use all the available tracking data and social media tools, but you will not get big results because the ingredient that ties them together is strategy—which brings you back to your message, your purpose, and the result you intend to get. These are the ingredients that win customers and leave them wanting more.

Here are two big-picture approaches to analyzing your web site and filtering the content for strategy and impact:

Is your web site active or passive? Does your site resemble a billboard invitation, or is it a smart package ready for delivery? We just assume that a site should invite visitors into our home page and welcome pages. But that model isn't always the best one. Sometimes you need a site that has been strategically wrapped to be quickly delivered and unwrapped exactly the way you intend.

What is your web site's persona? Is your site self-indulgent and all about your company? Or is it solution-oriented to the problems and expectations of customers? A common trend is to create sites that come across as big selfies. The graphics are huge and the content is full of self-aggrandizement, not only about *our* products and services, but about *our* staff—as though your team is the most unique group of people we'll ever meet.

The truth is, customers aren't interested in how much you like to play paint ball, or that you enjoy spending time with family. They want to know: what do you really do and how will it help *them*. That's where your focus should be and that's what you need to communicate.

Build a Creative Brief

The table on the next page is one example of key questions to ask yourself (or your client) prior to building a web site. The goal of a creative brief is to (1) capture the larger context of what the site needs to communicate and why, (2) ensure that the company branding and message are accurate and consistent, and (3) define a clear strategy for organizing and presenting the message to visitors.

Creative Brief for a Web Site
WHAT. What does your company do/provide for customers?
HOW. How do you do it? What is your approach, tools, skills?
WHY. Why are you in this business? What motivates you?
WHO. Who is behind the company? What are the *human* values?
1. Describe your company, products, and services.
2. What is the purpose/goal/intent of this web site?
3. What is working well with your current site?
4. What do you want to improve about your current site?
5. Are there any web sites you want to emulate? Why?
6. Who is your ideal target audience?
7. What core message do you want to convey?
8. Do you have a tagline or slogan?
9. What is your logo trying to convey?
10. What motivates customers to use your product or service?
11. What main *problem* do you solve for customers?
12. What tangible *solution* do you provide?
13. What intangible *value* do you provide?
14. Who are your main competitors?
15. What sets you apart from your competitors?
16. What main takeaway do you want visitors to carry with them?
17. What do you want the final call-to-action to be?
18. Any final thoughts or preferences?

- If you are building a web site for a client, send these questions to them as a starting point for discussion about your approach. *Listen* as much as possible. Create *their* vision of the site.

Write in a Circle

To make an end is to make a beginning.
The end is where we start from.
T.S. Eliot

From Chaos to Order

Writing is often messy, especially in the beginning. The same is true of all the arts. Where do you gather from? How do you start? What exactly are you trying to do?

The image below says it all: that it is possible to take a long strand of unorganized information and arrange it into something useful *and* beautiful that is ready to use with ease and precision—which is exactly what you want your communications to achieve.

Handing your readers a pile of rope is far different than placing in front of them a carefully organized coil that unfurls effortlessly in front of them.

Think in Steps of Three

This book has repeatedly emphasized that your main writing steps are: (1) plan with *precision*, (2) build themes around your *core message*, and (3) gear everything to achieve the *result* you want with the reader.

One way to bring all of these together is to envision them as three sections that together form the 'circle' of your communication.

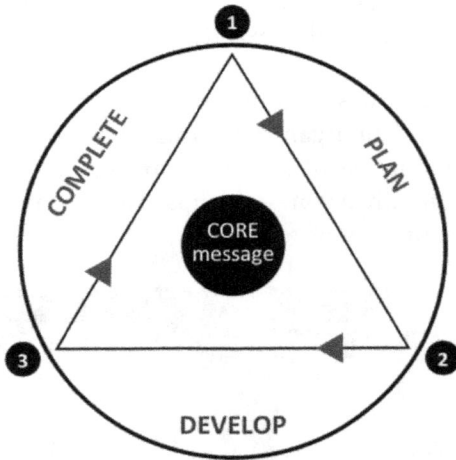

Your bow-and-arrow has now become a target with three sections and a bull's eye in the middle. This is a holistic view of your project, its direction, and its purpose.

Inside-out and Outside-in

In general, there are two ways you can think about organizing material as a finished product for the reader: inside-out and outside-in.

Inside-out

You can start at the inner core and work your way out while building a continuous circle of ideas that connect as they unfold into the larger whole of your message.

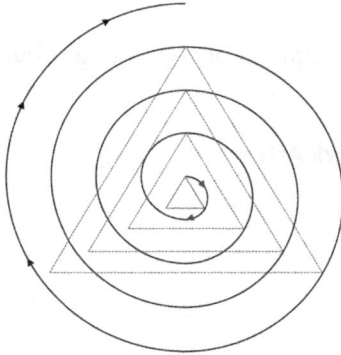

Outside-in

You can also start with the big picture and work your way in, getting increasingly specific about the detailed parts that comprise the whole.

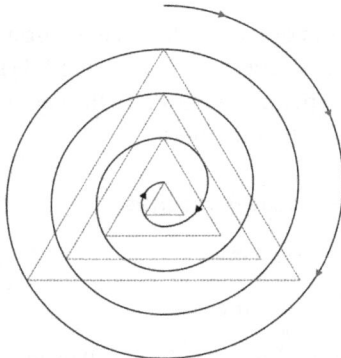

With both approaches, your core message serves as the unifying ingredient.

Build Each Step in 3 Parts

Whichever approach you take, break each main section of your circle into three steps of its own. Think of it as a modified version of A-I-D-A with the two middle parts (I and D) combined.

Here is one example of how you might build the steps in each section:

1. PLAN — spark Attention

1.   Introduce your topic.

2.   Make a statement related to your core message.

3.   Indicate where the document is headed.

2. DEVELOP — build Interest and Decision

1.   Introduce and promote each major theme.

2.   Explain how the theme is tied to your core message.

3.   Punctuate the theme's significance.

> NOTE: Think of the development section as a series of 3-step modules where each module introduces a new theme and ties it to the core message (as well as to other themes).

3. COMPLETE — focus Awareness

1.   Recapitulate the topic.

2.   Reaffirm the core message.

3.   Offer a conclusive thought, challenge, or inspiration.

This approach can serve as a blueprint for how to build, not only your entire document, but each section and each paragraph. It echoes the same principle of construction that you find in great music, literature, painting, dance, and architecture where chaos and content are organized through form and unity in an expression of beauty.

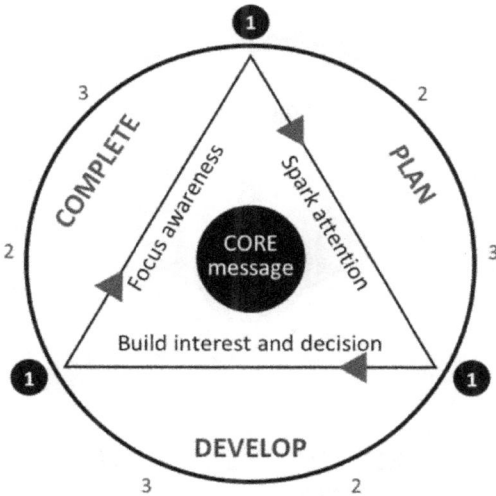

○ Breaking each main stage into 3 steps is a way to keep your work simple, clear, and organized. All you have to do is think in terms of 3 steps, no matter which stage (or which theme) you are working on. When you build each stage this way, they naturally merge into a fluid circle of strong, clear communication.

Understanding the Whole

Once you get accustomed to using a strategic approach to writing, you will realize that your *core* message is a condensation of your *whole* message, just as your whole message—all your sections, steps, and themes—is a *reflection* and expression of your core message.

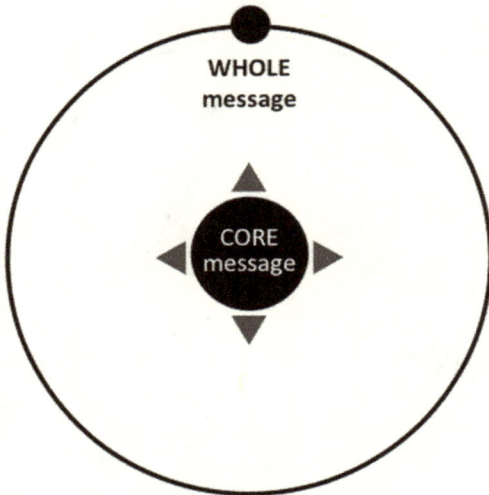

You will also learn that strategic writing is indeed a circle that rolls into itself, unrolls out of itself, and ends where it started—just as T.S. Eliot said.

As you start to feel the unity of design and construction behind your writing, and when you knowingly work to achieve it every time you write, you will reach the exciting threshold of mastering writing as both art and architecture.

Great RFPs and Responses

How to Improve the Proposal Process

Given the importance that RFPs play in the business world, it is surprising—especially with all the proposal writing methodologies that are espoused in the industry—how unprofessional and ineffective RFPs (and responses to them) continue to be. The truth is that no one likes how the process works, yet this is how it has worked for decades—largely due to imitation and an aversion to strategic planning.

The teams of program managers, project managers, and solution engineers who write RFPs are usually busy doing other critical work. Writing is not part of their primary job description, nor is it something that most of them enjoy. For this group, writing is a chore, a headache, and an unwelcome deviation.

The result is that RFPs end up being cobbled together, usually from existing material pulled from other projects. And because different people are assigned responsibility for different parts of an RFP, the document is often disjointed, poorly organized, and hard to decipher in both its parts and as a whole. What is sent to bidders is a complicated document assembled with high-school writing skills and difficult to understand, not to mention challenging to respond to—especially in a short amount of time.

Meanwhile, bidding teams are not always equipped to respond strategically, logistically, or quickly. They, too, cull content from previous responses and then re-use diagrams or graphics that they don't have the skill or time to adapt to each new bid. Their response ends up being a generic document which does little more than regurgitate the RFP and say "we can do the job." Very little strategy or creativity go into the process of crafting and delivering a powerful, persuasive, professional message. With this in mind, here are some key recommendations for preparing *and* responding to RFPs.

Chronic Problems with the RFP Process

The process of responding to RFPs is often confusing and stressful due to circumstances that both issuers and bidders have come to accept and tolerate. For example:

- An already tight response time is made tighter by delayed business-development (BD) decisions.

- Once a proposal team starts work, it frequently has no rehearsed strategy. Even when there is a strategy, it is often disregarded due to pressures of urgency.

- Also due to urgency, strategic tactics get glossed over in the rush to produce—to see—a first draft.

- Technical solutions are based on a loose interpretation of unclear guidelines.

- Content is usually copied and pasted from previous documents by people on different teams and different projects without the benefit of a qualified coordinator.

- The final product is 'good enough,' but rarely a superior demonstration of strategy, inventiveness, and tactical persuasion.

- Throughout the response process, confidence in the bid is generally not discussed. Everyone is in a hurry, under pressure, and not wanting to rock the boat by questioning whether the process is really working. Meanwhile, it is tacitly assumed that the burden of responsibility lies with bidders who believe (wrongly) that industry-standard methodologies are their best solution.

What if the problem—*and* the solution—lie on the RFP end? What if RFPs could be improved to make the response process more effective for bidders *and* more beneficial to issuers?

How Issuers Can Improve the Process

Companies who issue RFPs can also improve the process by creating RFP content that is easier for bidders to respond to, and easier for issuers to evaluate. With this in mind, here is some advice for issuers:

- Give up the notion that your RFP should be a challenge for bidders to diagnose and understand.

- Dispense with the need for a cover letter in the response. It is usually just a formality. Everyone knows who has issued the bid, what the title is, and that the bidder is grateful for the opportunity. Forego all that and move right to the problem and solution.

- Do away with formatting guidelines. Instead of providing elaborate instructions on how to respond, provide a template and style sheet organized exactly the way you want to see the response information.

- Build a response template that is a mirror image of your RFP and statement of work (SOW). Don't make things vague or confusing for bidders, and don't make bidders wrestle with inconsistencies (and gaps) that exist between the RFP guidelines and the SOW. Help make *their* solution easier to explain by making *your* requirements more clear. (Doing so will also make your evaluation process much easier.)

- Be clear about how many levels of hierarchy you want to see in the TOC so all response TOCs look the same at first glance (see example below).

- Include a predesigned cover page for the response that allows each bidder to insert their logo. Otherwise, all you need on the cover is the RFP title, and number, date, bidder info, and bidder logo.

- Build the response template in the form of 2-page modules based on the Sequential Thematic Organization of Proposals (S.T.O.P.) method that was first developed by project engineers at the Hughes Aircraft Corporation (more on this later).

- Require bidders to place all their content in 2-page modules regardless of how much content they have. Force them to compartmentalize according to your criteria (which will make your evaluation process easier, faster, and more comprehensive).

- Do not include evaluation criteria in the RFP. In other words, don't teach to the test. Let bidders assume that everything is important and will be weighed on its merits as part of the whole. Let them be responsible for demonstrating their full value, integrity, and experience.

- Specify page limits (module limits) and the maximum/minimum size for graphics as well as the number of graphics per module—which will limit the total number of graphics.

- Give bidders a realistic time frame for responding. Take into account that before your RFP gets to their writers, their business development (BD) team needs to receive it, review it, decide whether to bid, put it in their schedule queue, and do a kick-off.

- Discourage regurgitation of the RFP. Encourage bidders to focus on explaining how their solution will address your needs. Build a response template that is tailored to do exactly that.

- Provide a smarter RFP. If you want bidders to craft an authentic, intelligent response, you need to do the same with the RFP. The strategy, integrity, and thoroughness of your RFP will be the best test of the value of their response. *The more effort you put into crafting the RFP, the easier it will be to evaluate qualified responses.*

- Use the response template to strengthen your RFP. The exercise of putting together a strategic response template for bidders will greatly inform—and improve the quality of—your RFP.

How Bidders Can Improve the Process

Bidders can support the RFP process by examining and retooling their steps for receiving, processing, and responding to RFPs. Here is some advice for bidders:

- Tighten up BD quality control so that only RFPs with a realistic chance of success are bid on and so that RFPs reach the writing team ASAP.

- Stipulate decision-making guidelines to avoid the shotgun approach of bidding on everything. Adopt a sniper mentality that will save time and yield tangible ROI.

- Maintain a clear record of 'bid-no-bid' versus 'win' status. Use this as a guide for determining more exactly why, whether, and how best to bid.

- Expand BD to include the writing team so that everyone is on the same page from the get-go.

- Encourage your writers to be creative, explore options, and help problem-solve. The more you include writers in the big picture *from the beginning of the process,* the more understanding and creativity they will bring to the response. Conversely, the more you treat writers as small cogs in the wheel, the less interested and productive they will be.

- Scrutinize your response strategy so that you produce a concrete, solution-oriented, and value-packed response that reflects the customer's values as well as their needs—rather than a document that just touts your company *ad nausea.*

- Build a comprehensive response matrix and use it to storyboard. Format the matrix format so you can include (and easily see) every element of the response: due dates, contact info, special instructions, questions, comments, topics, value propositions, win themes, solution strategies, features, benefits, proof points, differentiators, your overall writing approach, each module framework, which graphics to include, who will write which section, etc.

- Put the customer in the foreground, your solution in the middle ground, and your company in the background. Let your understanding of customer needs and your vision of a solution reflect the merits of your company.

- Institute a playbook of steps for reviewing, breaking down, and evaluating RFPs so you are confident and in agreement about solutions, differentiators, and value-packed propositions.

- Do away with the drag of color-team reviews. Color teams frustrate and demoralize writers. Instead, use time up front to weigh strategies, to storyboard the entire response, and to get management buy-in on content and approach *before anyone starts writing.*

- Insist that anyone who gets to review or edit or approve drafts has to be involved from the beginning and throughout the entire response process.

- Minimize copying and pasting from previous responses. Don't make every proposal like the last one. Carefully edit copied content to ensure that it fits with the strategy of the current response.

- Dare to be different, innovative, and customer-focused. Remember: It's not about you. It's about the customer, their needs, and their values. Put as much attention as possible on *them* and *their* needs.

A Sample RFP Template

The table below is one example for building an RFP so that you get responses which are organized and formatted the same way so that they will be easier for you to read, compare, and evaluate. This example is simple, but it should give you a clear idea of how to think strategically when crafting your RFP. It is also just one example. You want to be flexible and construct your message to bidders in a way that suits your company culture, project, and needs. Don't simply follow industry standards for writing an RFP. Think about what you want and communicate that clearly to your bidders.

Sample Template

Sections (TOC)	Instructions/Questions to Bidders
Title Page	RFP title • Due date • Bidder info • Bidder logo
Understanding of Need	• Don't regurgitate the RFP. • Demonstrate your understanding of the problem/need. • Provide an overview of your solution.
Proposed Solution	• How will your solution specifically address our needs? • How do you envision project priorities? • Where do you anticipate problems? • What benefits will your solution provide?
Project Management	• Describe your overall PM approach. • How are your teams led, organized, and managed? • How will you measure and report progress? • How will you address issues that arise?
Project Team	• Who will be doing the work? • *(Provide a template for résumés and specify what bidders should include and not include, as pertinent to this project.)*
Past Performance	• What experience qualifies you for this project? *(Include in the template a table with the specific criteria you want bidders to include. Emphasize that you want them to describe similar completed projects and project achievements, not their approach.)*
Expertise and Innovation	• What distinguishes your team's skills, approach, creativity, and ingenuity? *(Explain that this is where bidders can differentiate themselves by showcasing additional talent, tools, and approach.)*

Pricing (separate package)	• Use the attached templates to build your pricing information. *(Provide a prepared table, spreadsheet, and/or PM chart for bidders to complete so the information is displayed exactly the way you want to see it for evaluation and scoring, and so that pricing information from all vendors has the same layout and formatting.)*
Administrative Requirements (separate package)	• Include company and staff certifications, QC plan, safety plan, risk management plan, insurance, warranties, etc. *(Provide in the template a placeholder and checklist for these attachments. Clarify any special requirements.)*
Evaluation Criteria (separate package)	• Include specific descriptions of how and why evaluation scoring will be measured. • *Alternatively*, don't provide any evaluation criteria. Make everything important.

Use Modules When Writing Responses

The 2-page module was devised by engineers at the Hughes Aircraft Corporation when they were swamped with writing proposal responses (bids) for military contracts during the Cold War. They wanted an efficient method that would bring more control, consistency, and success to their process of preparing proposals. They called it the Sequential Thematic Organization of Publications (S.T.O.P.) method. By strictly adhering to the 2-page module for each theme, they made their writing more concise and their message (their understanding of the problem and their proposed solutions) *much* easier to understand. In the process, they won a whole lot of contracts over a short span of time.

For some reason, this highly effective technique went out of fashion or was forgotten—probably because it is too simple *and* because it requires a lot of focused thinking to consolidate and streamline information in well wrapped containers. Compared to the S.T.O.P. method, today's proposals are a disappointment because they are poorly engineered, challenging to read, and difficult to comprehend. The reason is that they *lack* the following:

- Strategy

- Clarity

- Unity

- Core message

- Topic interest

- Human interest

- Ease of reader usability

By contract, proposals that are engineered with 2-page modules (one module per theme) include all of the things just listed above. And because they do, they tend to be:

- Simple

- Strategic

- Persuasive

- Compelling

- A pleasure to read

- Broken into clear parts *and* unified as a whole

- Easy to unwrap and understand

These ingredients are achieved by building each module using the same organizational strategy and format so that every theme fits into a side-by-side page design. Doing this breaks your message into consistent, simple-to-chew parts that are easy to understand and easy to remember—all of which have enormous impact on the reader.

The basic formula for writing modules

Here is a simple recipe for using the modular approach to writing:

- Break your proposal into major topics.

- Establish key themes for each topic.

- Build a 2-page module for each theme.

- Don't stray beyond 2 pages per theme.

- Don't feel you have to 'fill up' every module.

Take a few minutes to study the example on the following pages. Notice how succinct and definitive this approach can be. Try to grasp the fundamental approach while considering how you might use this tool and modify it to meet *your* needs.

Sample Module — Left-hand Page

Section: #   **Topic**: title

Theme Heading

Thesis statement. Write a concise sentence (or two) to convey the core element of what this module theme covers and why it is important. The thesis statement should captivate readers with a key point of interest that entices them to keep reading.

Expand. Expand and develop the theme with 3 to 5 additional sentences. Add specific data, measures, goals. Avoid fluff about your company. Focus on the theme and its relevance to the customer's needs.

Prove. Give concrete examples that show (not just tell) your team's expertise and your company's experience with implementing this theme/solution successfully and cost efficiently.

Differentiate. Specify how your experience ties directly to the topic of this theme and why your approach/solution demonstrates value and merits special consideration.

(Limit your 2-page spread to 750 words + graphic)

Sample Module — Right-hand Page

Right-hand (odd-numbered) page

Section: #   **Topic**: title

Features. Highlight the *exact* problem (related to this theme) that you will be solving and the unique features your solution will provide.

Benefits. Clarify *how* (not what) the client will benefit from your solution. Address end results and ROI.

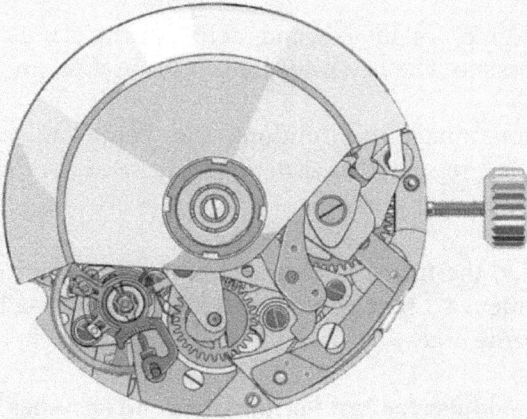

Punctuate. Include a strong image with an active caption that emphasizes this theme.

Tips When Building Modules

- Use bold to highlight the first few words, or even the entire first sentence, of a paragraph—as a way to emphasize key points that readers can scan quickly, dive into, and find easily.

- Pay special attention to your thesis statement. It is the core of each module.

- Write paragraph leads as *active-voice* statements.

- Keep graphics, images, and tables as simple and clear as possible. The best ones explain *themselves* quickly.

- Use *one* image that reinforce the theme's message. *And use images that actually make sense and communicate your point.*

- Ideally, the image echoes and punctuates the thesis statement so that you start, build, and end—all on the same note.

Use Modules for Past Performance and Résumés

It is important how you present, and how clearly you present, your solution. It is equally important that you make the rest of your proposal clear and persuasive. This includes your past performance and résumés of proposed staff, both of which you can also present as one- or two-page modules.

✪ Make all résumés look the same (font, format, organization). Highlight the skills/experience that are relevant to the job in question. Do this in a special section (such as a text box or table) on each résumé. *Don't expect evaluators to read every line of every résumé.*

Why Modules Work

Modules are as powerful as proposal writing gets. Instead of sending clients a long, complicated, disjointed document that they have to struggle to unravel, you will be sending them a large box full of clearly delineated packages that are easy (even a pleasure) to unwrap and read. Modular proposals also make it easy for evaluation teams to check your document quickly, locate information, and do a final analysis. All your key points will stand out and be easy to find. Evaluators will be left with a strong impression of your company's tight organization, strategic message, and expert mindset.

Three components often determine whether you will win a bid:

1. Who you know.

2. Your pricing.

3. The caliber of your proposal.

The third can go a long way toward swaying the first two and may make the difference, especially when the choice is between you and one other company. A strategically organized, clearly written, polished proposal is a statement of 'integrity', 'quality', and 'responsibility'—all of which make you stand out among the competition.

✪ The final, often overlooked reason why module writing is so effective is that it builds skill and confidence *in your writers and in your company as a whole.* The better you can articulate what you do, why you do it, what distinguishes it, and how it benefits your customers, the more your employees will want to work with you and the more your customers will want to do business with you.

Managing Large Writing Projects

Note: This section is intended primarily for business and technical writers who manage large documents and/or writing teams.

The Project Process

A well organized writing project is easy is to manage. But without a clear process, the happy ship of writing plunges into extensive rewriting, scheduling conflicts, budget problems, forced deadlines, and endless changes. If and when the document resurfaces, its readability usually bears witness to a chaotic lifecycle. Even with a strong process, the document lifecycle can be fickle. Requirements change unexpectedly. New material gets added. Bureaucratic decisions stall your progress.

A clear process helps all of these things. It makes a document easier to write and manage. In most cases it charts a safe course, calms the administrative waters, and stems the tide of problems. Even when a project gets put on hold, having a reliable process makes it easy to pick up where you left off instead of having to start over.

Process Pitfalls to Watch For

Here are some common pitfalls in the writing process. Watch for them and be prepared to avoid them.

- **Vague planning**. Resist the urge to hurry into writing. It is always tempting to start writing without planning. Understand, however, that planning cannot take place *after* you have started writing—no matter how much rewriting you do.

- **Lack of focus**. The most common weakness of documents is their lack of message and direction. Not enough time is devoted to analyzing the topic, distilling the core message, and determining the best strategy for reaching the reader. The result is a lack of vitality, crispness, and comprehension.

- **Going off track**. Wandering text is usually the result of a weak outline or of not using the outline as a guide for writing. To avoid this, analyze and plan until you feel extremely confident about your message, organization, and strategy—*then* start writing. Keep the outline in front of you while you write and check it often for alignment.

- **Waiting for perfection**. Writers are almost never satisfied because they know there is another way, possibly a better way, to say what they have said. But at some point you have to step back and let the document go. The important thing is: does it deliver (with impact) the message you intended?

Writing a Project Proposal Before You Write

One way to organize a writing project is to write a proposal for it. A project proposal is a summary of the proposed document: its topic, strategy, message, and key elements. The purpose of a project proposal is to show team members, managers, and clients (even professors) the ingredients and strategy of what you intend to write.

A proposal paves the way for cooperation and prevents misunderstandings before they develop. It gets everyone thinking in tandem by stating things clearly from the beginning.

Writing projects often start and develop without clear consensus. Team members have different concepts about the purpose and strategy, yet these differences never get discussed. A project proposal remedies this by clarifying all the elements beforehand.

A project proposal should be part of the planning stage. Once it is approved, you can move quickly to development. On the other hand, if a proposal is rejected or postponed, you have not wasted time on unnecessary writing.

Whether you are a manager, writer, author, or student, your project proposal should answer these questions:

- Why is this document being written?

- What will it achieve?

- How long will it take?

- (and often) How much will it cost?

Key Elements of a Project Proposal

A project proposal may be one or one hundred pages long, depending on your need and requirements. The following steps, however, are essential to proposals of any size:

- **Define the concept**. What is the general idea behind the proposed document? How did it come about? What is the rea-son(s) for doing it? You would think this is obvious, and because this is a common assumption, the central idea is usually glossed over in everyone's mind. No time and effort is devoted to a healthy discussion: What are we really doing here? Why are we bothering to put in all this work? How do er intend to use this document as a tool? Many good ideas and rationale and strategic inventive-ness never come to the surface because they are not given a chance to. If they were, these initial discussions can bear a lot of fruit and arouse a lot of creativity in the minds of managers and especially in the writers who will be actually crafting the document, building the tool, and delivering the message.

- **Describe the topic**. What is the main subject? What are the key points?

- **Pinpoint the core message**. In one sentence, what central message is being delivered to the reader? What core idea will everything else revolve around?

- **Profile the reader**. Who is the primary reader? What essential information does the reader need? What level of familiarity with the topic does the reader have? What is the best way to deliver the message to this reader?

- **Explain the result**. What problem will the document solve? What questions will it answer? What key benefits will it provide? What other outcomes will the document produce?

- **Provide an outline**. Include at least a three-tiered outline (I-A-1). Include a sketch outline if you want to show the logic behind your initial brainstorming. Include a task outline, table outline, or storyboard if you also want to show how the document will take shape.

- **Provide summaries**. Include a section summary for each major section of the proposed document. Do this especially if you think it will reinforce your justification for the project.

- **Prepare a time/cost estimate**. In the business world, projects boil down to time and money. In this case, provide a reasonable time period for how long you think it will take and how much it may cost. Make it clear that these are estimates and that exact numbers will be provided later.

- **Show the development stages**. Include a copy of your 7-step document development process. Show your manager, client, or professor how you intend to build the document in stages. Let them see that you have full command of the process.

Use a Project Proposal To Say 'No'

A project proposal can also help you say 'no' to something that is not feasible. Use the guidelines above to show why an idea does *not* make sense, or is not defined clearly enough, or is too ambitious for a given budget.

Keep a Project Chart

A project chart is a profile of your document and a checklist for completing it. Like a medical chart, it monitors progress. It helps you track, at every step, what has been done and what lies ahead.

Use a project chart to explain the scope of a project and show exactly where it is in the development lifecycle. This is a tool for staying organized and for communicating with managers and clients. If you lead a team of writers, a project chart also becomes a way for them to keep you informed of their progress.

A project chart is an excellent tool for preliminary discussions and interviews. The full spectrum of a project can be examined from the beginning. All aspects can be recorded and thought about. Each project can be approached in the same professional way.

Develop a project chart that suits your project and works for you. Keep it up to date. Post it where others can see it physically or access it electronically.

Project

| Name | Start Date: | Due Date: |
| Leader | Client Contact: | |

Scope

Concept

Intended Reader & Result

Proposed Budget

Materials Needed

Graphics Needed

Printing Specs

Special Attention

Review Team

Notes

Checklist

- ☐ Concept defined
- ☐ Topic analysis
- ☐ Sketch outline
- ☐ Topic outline
- ☐ Topics to tasks
- ☐ Page model
- ☐ Storyboard
- ☐ Cost estimate
- ☐ Project proposal
- ☐ Section summaries
- ☐ Paragraph briefs
- ☐ Style sheet / template
- ☐ Draft 1   ☐ Edit
- ☐ Draft 2   ☐ Edit
- ☐ Final   ☐ Edit
- ☐ Master   ☐ Saved

Communicate With Customers

Work closely with writers. If you are a team leader, support your writers by explaining the strategy behind each document. This will give them confidence and focus. It is easy for everyone to assume they will approach a writing project the way you intend, but it is rarely true. Therefore, communicate the topic, purpose, core message, and intended result before anyone starts writing.

When discussing strategies with writers, keep meetings short. Twenty minutes is plenty of time if you know what you want. More than an hour is too long because details get confusing and dullness sets in. Long meetings lose their impact. Short meetings convey clarity, purpose, and goals, which is exactly what you want to carry over into writing.

Another way to use team meetings is to ask instead of tell. What do the writers think the strategy should be? What is their sense of the core message and purpose? Do they have ideas for planning or organizing the document? Writers will love you for asking these kind of questions. It appeals directly to their sense of themselves as writers. It also promotes their interest and creativity.

Allow writers time to think about these questions and respond with their own ideas. Encourage invention. Let them spark a project and help make it successful.

Keep clients informed. Clients also like to know what is going on with their projects. And they frequently want to be part of the process, so keep them informed and ask for their feedback.

One of the best ways to keep clients informed is to ask for their feedback at the beginning of a project. Show them your bow-and-arrow analysis. Let them review the outline. Present a storyboard before you start writing. Explaining your document development method will bolster their confidence in your business skills.

Outlines and storyboards are a useful way to prepare clients for seeing full drafts. Instead of receiving a large unknown draft, they will be already familiar with the subject matter. They will have a handle on the strategy, the structure, and the organization. They will be better acclimated and their reviews will be more effective.

Another way to support clients is to instruct them about how to review outlines, storyboards, and drafts. Describe what you need. Tell them about what to look for and how to respond. In other words, manage their feedback so that it comes back to you in consistent, usable form.

Use Status Reports

Status reports are usually mentioned at the beginning of a project and then either forgotten or underused as the project develops. This is unfortunate because a good status report can have many uses for you, your team members, and your clients.

A common weakness of status reports is abbreviated writing (incomplete sentences) and impersonal tone. Try to resist these tendencies. Provide full information. Explain things clearly. Give examples of what you mean.

Projects differ in scope, but a good rule of thumb is to limit status reports to one page. Doing so will help you focus on key issues and highlight the most critical items.

Over the course of a project, a series of status reports becomes a profile of progress. This is useful for existing projects and as a reference when planning future projects. You will be surprised how helpful it can be to refer back to well written status reports.

Design each status report to suit each project. Ask team members and clients what information they want to see. Explain that you intend to use status reports as a communication link to keep the project focused and moving. Encourage everyone to actually read and respond to them in a spirit of participation.

Status Report   **Date:**

Project Name	Text
Project Manager	Text
Estimated Completion	Text
Time Remaining	Text
Recent Work Completed	Text
Notable Achievements	Text
Existing Issues	Text
Items of Interest	Text
Next Work Scheduled	Text
This Report Sent To	Text
Prepared By	Text

Manage the Review Cycle

A thorough review of the document by team members, managers, and clients is crucial to its success. The review process, however, is frequently a weak link in the development lifecycle. One reason is because reviewers are busy doing their main job. A document that needs to be reviewed can lie fallow on their desk for days or weeks, quietly delaying an entire project.

Another weak spot in the review process is a lack of clarity about how it will work and what everyone needs to do. For instance, writers expect reviewers to give their documents priority and provide the feedback they need. Reviewers, on the other hand, assume they know how to review documents, and they expect writers to respect their recommendations. Rarely, however, do things turn out the way everyone expects.

A third problem is the form in which review comments come back to writers. In many cases, each reviewer uses his own method of responding, so writers end up with an inconsistent set of comments to incorporate. Many writers would probably agree that one of their most unpleasant tasks is having to address inconsistent suggestions from a large variety of reviewers.

One solution to all these problems is to establish review-cycle guidelines for everyone. Discuss guidelines ahead of time. Explain why they are useful. Ask for everyone's cooperation. When reviewers feel the importance of their role and understand what is required, they respond much better and you can get back to writing.

✪ Send instructions with each review. Reiterate what you expect and need for that review, and how reviewers can best respond. Otherwise, each reviewer will respond in his own way.

Suggested Guidelines for Reviews

- **Turnaround time**. Set a time limit for each review. Three days is ideal; it keeps things fresh and moving forward. Seven days is a good maximum. Beyond that interest wanes, the sense of purpose gets lost, and a project falls into limbo.

- **Options**. If reviewers don't like being pressed for time, give them options. For example, ask for a three-day turnaround. As a second option, ask for seven days. As a third option, let reviewers know that comments returned after 10 days will not be incorporated unless the reviewer calls ahead of time for an extension. Explain that the project needs to move forward with their help. Don't bully. Appeal for support.

- **Instructions**. Instead of waiting for reviewers to establish their own guidelines, explain what information you need and how they can provide it. For instance, if they are reviewing the outline, explain that you need feedback about its organization and sequence. For section summaries and paragraph briefs, ask reviewers to confirm or clarify the main points. For the first draft, ask for improvements to the sequence and flow of writing. Does it make sense? Is the core message being delivered?

- **Follow up**. After each review, let reviewers know that you received their comments and appreciate them. Ask for clarification on any points that are still in question.

✪ At the end of a project, send a thank-you memo to everyone. Set a positive tone for future projects.

Estimate Time and Cost

Calculating how long it will take to finish a document and how much it will cost often depends on how long the document will be. Page length is hard enough to gauge when you have all the content (notes, memos, research data, and graphics). It is even harder when you don't have them.

Ideally, you receive a request, respond with a project proposal, then develop a plan, create a schedule, and build the document. But you rarely have this luxury. If you are a business or technical writer, you are usually given a broadly defined task and a deadline, with the deadline being the most important. You are expected to fit the document into the schedule, rather than the other way around. Here are some things that can help:

Time Estimates for One Page

The numbers on the following age are fairly common standards for estimating development time (planning, development, and completion) for one page. They are based on averages and assume that the writer will also be creating the graphics.

- Basic text (no graphics)   4 hrs. per page

- Complex text (no graphics)   5 hrs. per page

- Text with one graphic   6 hrs. per page

- Complex text with one graphic   7 hrs. per page

- Very complex text with graphics   8 hrs. per page

- Specialized text with graphics 9 hrs. per page

- Detailed format and graphics 10 hrs. per page

These averages give you a little (not a lot) of extra room. They will vary depending on the project and how you work. They include the total time required for planning, outlining, writing, editing, review, and final production of one page.

If you want to be more conservative (which is a good idea until you gain confidence in your estimating skills), add ten percent to your final estimate. If you are an independent contractor, add twenty percent. Keep in mind that it is always better to overestimate and then finish a project early and under budget than to miss the deadline and accrue extra costs.

✪ If you are *not* developing the graphics, remember that you need to create placeholders for them in the document, then import them, resize them, and perhaps edit them. These tasks will affect your hour and page counts.

Convert Hours to Pages and Stages

Convert hours to pages. When you are given a deadline, the best approach is to determine the number of work days available for the project. For instance, suppose you have 60 work days to complete a document. Taking eight hours per day as a basis, 60 days converts to 480 hours. The conversion to pages would be as follows:

- 480 hrs. @ 4 hrs. per page = 120 pages

- 480 hrs. @ 6 hrs. per page = 80 pages

- 480 hrs. @ 8 hrs. per page = 60 pages

Using this formula (or one like it), determine the page limit and establish that as your project boundary. This may seem restricting but it will give you a feasible target.

Although this approach is somewhat backwards, it works. You simply let the project requirements drive your development lifecycle. As long as everyone understands this strategy, it works well—even though you will be required to squeeze the absolute most out of your document plan, time, and resources.

Convert hours to development stages. When estimating development time, many people put too much emphasis on development (writing and editing) and not enough on planning (core message and outlines). The result is superficial planning and sloppy follow-through.

Rapid development should not supersede planning. Be professional. Make sure that development grows out of planning. One technique is to aim to finish a document (as though you were going to press) 10 days ahead of schedule. This gives you time to tie up loose ends and make last-minute corrections.

Here is one suggestion for allotting time to the different stages of development:

- Strategy (core, reader, purpose, result)   10 percent

- Outlines (sketch, topics, tasks)   20 percent

- Blueprint (page modules, template)   10 percent

- Content (summaries and briefs)   20 percent

- First draft 25 percent

- Final draft 10 percent

- Print and finish   5 percent

Mark these time and percentage estimates on your project chart, communicate them to everyone involved, and try to stick to them. If you are unsure, at least mark them on your own calendar and try to stick to them personally.

If you encounter problems and delays during development, record this information for future use. Each project is different. Paying close attention to how the development cycle unfolds will sharpen your project management skills for next time.

Advice for Program Managers

Give writers the freedom to manage your department's writing projects, including content, strategy, design, and the review process. Support writers by letting *them* be in charge of the result. As part of this, eliminate color reviews (which stifle writers by sending a message of "this is broken, fix it"). Instead, get stakeholders involved in the strategy and planning stages *from the beginning.*

Writing Grants

The Grant Picture

You need a source of funds to support your vision. *They* want a donation vehicle that reflects their values.

You Need

- Source of funds
- Actualize your vision
- Recurring support

They Want

- Donation vehicle
- Reflect their values
- A partnership

The **standard** approach is to tout your organization while justifying the need for money.

The **strategic** approach is to put your organization in the shoes of the funding source and explain *your* vision in the light of *their* values.

The **bottom line** is that you want to *align* your application to the funding source in every way possible. It is about you, but it is always more about addressing their goals.

Requesting Funds and Responding to Grants

Even though you are the organization asking for money, the focus of your message should not be about you. That sounds counterintuitive, but the reality is that your message should revolve not around you but around the vision and values of the funding source. Yes, you want to underscore why your organization is the best choice. But you also don't want to overhype your eligibility at the expense of acknowledging the integrity and goals of the funder. The balance you want to strike is to explain how your needs and project fit into their vision and goals. To do that, here are a few points to concentrate on as you build the strategy and content of your application response:

- **Think partnership**. If your organization gets selected to receive funds, it will be in large part because the funding source thinks you can be, and wants you to be, a reflection of its values. The relationship is not going to end with you simply getting a check. You will be reporting progress, submitting ongoing financial data, and staying on good terms. So you need to be thinking long term as a potential partner—which you will be in the sense that you will be putting *their* money to use in a way that echoes and reinforces *their* profile as a philanthropic entity.

- **Earn trust**. The usual tendency is for non-profits to emphasize their own accomplishments and needs, which is appropriate but which can come across as a *justification* of suitability. Remember, you are not trying to sell your services or win a company's business. You are trying to strike the right psychological nerve in the funding source. Do you align with their culture and vision? Will you be a responsible representative of that culture and vision? Can they depend on you to match their integrity and purpose? Will you be a good extension and reflection *of them?*

- **Distinguish yourself.** Everyone wants to highlight their past success and accolades, and doing so has its place. But you don't want to come across as a cocky, arrogant, superior-minded competitor. You want to demonstrate *through the tone of your message* what distinguishes and differentiates you as a potential partner. You are pitching character and results as much as need and deservedness.

- **Use research to write.** Don't jump into a grant application after just a quick look at the qualifications. Do as much research as you can on the funding source. Who is behind the original vision? Is it an individual, a family, a trust, a corporation? How much can you learn about their vision and human values? What can you learn about their philanthropic proclivities, the types of organizations they have helped, the kinds of projects they favor? Is there anything about your organization that seems to stand out as a special fit with theirs? Is there any reason why your organization might *not* be a good fit? Take elaborate notes and use them to consolidate and craft your narrative when responding. Demonstrate to the funder how well you understand their history and vision and values.

- **Narrow your aim.** Another tendency of organizations seeking funding is to compete for every grant they come across. Resist this urge. Focus instead on the most viable, most realistic, and most compatible partnerships. This will give you the time to plan a clear strategy and hone your message around it. It will also allow you to write an original, thoughtful narrative for each application instead of copying and pasting and tweaking. You want each response to be as authentic and convincing as possible.

✪ It is not called an 'award' or 'reward' or 'contract'. It is called a 'grant' which means it is money being allowed for you to use. Grantors take pride and honor in giving you their funds, and they like requests that reciprocate with respect, understanding, and appreciation, not only for the money but for the opportunity to participate and cooperate in the funder's goodwill and vision.

Extra Writing Tips

Learn to love white (empty) space

- White space is your friend, not your enemy.

- White space draws attention to what *remains*.

- White space creates a sense of calm and confidence.

- White space *allows* the reader to comprehend better.

False: Less is not more; it's less.

True: Less means less distraction and more impact.

False: We need to include as much information as possible.

True: You need to include only what reinforces your core message. Everything else is off target and a deviation.

False: Minimizing words and page elements makes a document appear incomplete and uninteresting.

True: Minimizing words and page elements forces you to strip down to your core message and deliver *that*.

Aim for Simple

Simple is hard because it makes you bore into just a few—sometimes only one—criteria that defines what your company does or will do for the client.

It's startling how many companies don't know what their core strength is and cannot articulate it in simple language—which is why they often use (lots of) words as camouflage instead of to communicate their real value.

Simple is fun because once you *do* understand your main offering and your core message and can explain them, your message becomes clearer, your brand stronger, and your customers more loyal.

False: Adding complexity will help us appeal to a wider market and bring in more business.

True: Going simple forces you to define your real value and the target audience who needs and wants it.

Each web site is a puzzle

Here are 4 tips for solving your puzzle:

- **Drop**. Dump all the pieces on the table. It's a mess. It seems daunting because the outcome is unknown at the beginning.

- **Sort**. Don't do random. Sort and organize first. Most importantly, find the central piece around which everything else can be assembled.

- **Resist**. Here's *the* key point: to find your core, you have to resist the urge to 'build' and 'expand' your site. Everyone wants to start building right away, usually by imitating someone else's puzzle and solution. Find your core first. Then assemble around that *slowly*.

- **Strip**. With all the pieces sorted in front of you, strip your puzzle down to its barest, simplest necessities. Be brutal. Then build gradually and watch it reveal itself.

The basic elements of every web site

1. **Strategic Planning & Organization.** *The blueprint* for brand impact, target audience, and intended results, designed tactically for easy unwrapping.

2. **Thematic Content.** *The core message* rolled out as themes that steer and unify all your content, built for simplicity, clarity, and ease of comprehension.

3. **Design.** *Visual statements* that accentuate your brand and your core message, and echo your solutions.

4. **Coding.** *The structural framework and engine* built to maximize and maintain 1-2-3.

✪ The best sites are built in the order 1-2-3-4 because each successive element should reinforce the ones preceding it.

✪ A common mistake is to build in the order 3-4-2-1.

✪ Another common mistake is when clever design elements distract from strategy and content rather than echo and reinforce them.

Learn to sketch

Sketching before you start writing is a powerful habit to develop. But why don't more writers sketch different approaches and tactics.? Because it requires time and thought, and it can feel as though you are wasting time. The technique of sketching preliminary writing ideas is also something that is neither taught nor encouraged.

But consider the following:

- Leonardo da Vinci did multiple studies, sketches, and under-paintings before he committed to final designs, compositions, perspectives, and colors.

- Dostoevsky took a stab at different plots and points of view before *Crime and Punishment* adopted the voice of a roving narrator who takes us into each character's mind.

- Great architects do lots of messy drawings and make-shift models before they finalize a blueprint.

✪ Sketching is a preparatory tool. A warm up.

✪ Sketching grants you freedom, flexibility, and fresh-ness.

✪ Sketching saves you from endless reorganization and rewriting.

Think *and* talk before you write

It is surprising how many writing teams assume an outcome and never (ever) discuss their projects or project assignments with each other.

Here are some simple questions that should always be asked and discussed among a team:

- Who is our *audience*—our one ideal reader?

- What do they *need* that we can provide?

- What is our focus—our core *message*?

- What *result* do we want/expect from this effort?

- What *process* are we going to follow when writing?

- Do we all agree on the *strategy* and *approach*?

- Who is going to *lead* the writing effort?

Don't color your world (review process)

The idea of color teams performing multiple reviews of a document has become popular with business development managers, but writers don't like color reviews because it undermines their work. Color reviews also *defeat* the process of strategic writing. Why? Because strategy is about building from the beginning, not fixing at the end.

✪ Anyone who is expected to be involved in the review stages of a document should be required to take part in the original strategy and planning, and even in some of the writing.

Never hand a building already in progress to someone who has not helped create the blueprint—unless you want just their first-impression reaction. Never give them the leverage to make strategic or structural changes after your writing team has already hammered out those stages.

Empower small teams

Contrary to popular business belief, it doesn't take 10 or 12 or 15 people to write a large document. Evidence shows that too many chefs (authors) leads to a messy kitchen and a ruined dish.

Small teams of subject matter experts guided by a talented writer take pride in being granted the autonomy to craft their documents. That is their job. It is why you hired them. And when they are left to do it, the result is often a dish with considerably more appeal than a dish concocted by a group of administrators and technicians.

✪ Executive leadership sees risks where project team members see opportunities. Which direction does your company pursue?

✪ Let your writers do their job.

Show the reader where you want to go

It may seem obvious to you, but it is often a problem for the reader who tends to ask (about a web site, a report, a proposal): What is this actually about? What is it really offering? What is the main point and solution?

To remedy this, build your message using the three tactics below, which you can either highlight for the reader *or* use as part of your underlying structure:

- **Where are we?** Clarify where the situation or problem now stands. What characterizes it today?

- **Where do we want to go?** Explain how it can be better. Draw a clear picture of your 'tomorrow'.

- **How do we get there?** This is your solution, your bridge, your value. Be specific and definite. Prove and persuade. End with impact.

✪ An added value of this tactical approach is that it demonstrates to the reader your knowledge, forethought, and confidence.

Develop your own writing process

Large writing projects—particularly proposals on which lots of dollars hinge—can seem intimidating. The 'experts' sound like they have it under control and so you think you should do it their way, use their methods, pay for their training.

But is that true? Why can't you develop a method suited to your company, your clients, your products, and your services? After all, you are the expert in your field.

The fact is that most people don't want to go through the agony of being strategic. They want someone else to give them the 'right' formula, which is why so many business communications end up looking like large housing developments where all the designs (formats) and floor plans (organization) are the same. There is no custom living! And the reading is dull. But it doesn't have to be that way.

✪ Don't be afraid to build your own process, to experiment with it, and to perfect it.

Include strategy at every step

Strategy is not something you do only at the beginning of a writing project. It is an *entire* approach.

There is a saying that "everything you do is marketing." In other words, marketing isn't reserved for moments of advertising and publicity. It includes all the little things, such as how you treat your team members, the tone of each email you send, whether you say thank you or not. The same is true about writing strategy. The more conscious you are of the tactic behind each paragraph, how you put it together, why you choose to present the information in a certain order, what effect you want it to have on the reader—*all* of these play a part. Together they make the difference between writing and strategic writing.

✪ Business writing and business communication often fall flat because the ingredient of strategy is missing, not only in the beginning but throughout the entire delivery of a message.

Strategic writers wear many hats

Good writing shares a lot in common with constructing and selling a home. Here are the many duties of an effective writer or writing team:

- Have a strategy (visionary).

- Turn your vision into a blueprint (architect).

- Plan and lay a solid foundation (engineer).

- Organize your content and team (contractor).

- Assemble a framework of ideas (carpenter).

- Connect the behind-the-scenes details (electrician).

- Make sure everything flows (plumber).

- Refine headings and images (finish craftsmen).

- Proof and polish the final version (painter).

- Convince the reader (realtor).

✪ All of the above call for a different mindset and different 'tools' of writing.

Show interest in your client

The client is often not that interested in you, but highly values you when you:

- Show that you understand the client's motives.

- Appeal to the client's specific needs.

- Present solutions, not *by* you, but *for* the client.

- Place you and your company in the background.

- Keep acknowledging the client as the main concern.

- Speak as an ambassador for your client's case.

✪ It takes constant practice to keep turning the focus repeatedly onto clients, *their* needs, and *their* solutions.

'Preventative' is a noun, not an adjective

Preventative is a noun: (a remedy that slows or prevents an illness).

Example: The doctor suggested several *preventatives.*

Preventive is an adjective: (intended to prevent or hinder).

Example: We practice *preventive* maintenance to avoid breakdowns.

✪ In almost all cases, preventive is the word you are looking for.

Use one space after a period or colon

Typing two spaces after a period is a habit carried over from letter-press printing and the typewriter when you had to add an extra space to visually delineate each sentence.

With the advent of desktop publishing and digital fonts, the double space became unnecessary.

✪ Every major style guide prescribes a single (one) space after the period as well as after all other punctuation, *including the colon.*

Don't use 'utilize'

In its correct form, utilize means "to turn to profitable account," such as when you utilize a stream to power a mill. In most cases, you 'use' software, equipment, and systems.

'Utilize' has a government/military ring to it and tends to be incorrect. 'Use' is simple, clear, and accurate.

- *Utilize* MS Word when writing documents.

- Our company *utilizes* the most effective management techniques.

✪ Avoid 'utilize' in almost all situations.

- *Use* MS Word when writing documents.

- Our company *uses* the most effective management techniques.

Avoid 'located in'

'In' already implies location.

- My office is *located in* Building 9.

- Dallas is *located in* Texas.

✪ Just write 'in'.

- My office is in Building 9.

- Dallas is in Texas.

Say "no" to 'in order to'

'In order to' is extraneous.

- *In order to* get there, you have to turn around.

- She hurried *in order to* be on time.

✪ Just write 'to'.

- To get there, you have to turn around.

- She hurried to be on time.

■

✪

About the Author

Peter Ingle specializes in strategic communications for business, government, and technology clients.

Consulting and Workshops

strategicbusinesswriters.com